From Small Town to Big Dreams

Luciana Fistarol

From Small Town to Big Dreams

50 LESSONS FROM A PROSPEROUS DIGITAL NOMAD

Luciana Fistarol

From Small Town to Big Dreams

First published in 2023

Print: 978-1-76124-116-1
E-book: 978-1-76124-115-4

Publishing information
Publishing and design facilitated by Passionpreneur Publishing
A division of Passionpreneur Organization Pty Ltd
ABN: 48640637529

Melbourne, VIC | Australia
www.PassionpreneurPublishing.com

From Small Town to Big Dreams

"I don't need a magic carpet to soar or wings to fly.
I simply close my eyes and place my soul against the sky."

— Melody Lee (Author of Moon Gypsy)

This book is dedicated to everyone who yearns to explore and paint on the vast canvas of this world. It is meant for those who want to push their potential to the fullest, to build a life and career more beautiful than their wildest dreams.

I would like to thank my parents.

My mother's open-mindedness has been instrumental in granting me the freedom to pursue my insatiable wanderlust. Without her, I would never have had the opportunity to embark on thrilling adventures and explore new horizons.

Equally important, my father's unwavering support has given me the strength and courage to embrace change and forge new paths.

And I would like to thank you, dear reader, for picking up this book. I hope it serves you well for all the wonderful adventures yet to come.

DIARY ENTRY 1

The Deepest Roots, for the Highest Heights

Stranger: *"Hey, nice to meet you! Where are you from?"*
Me: *"Hey! Apiuna."*
Stranger: *"What?"*
Me: *"I'm from Apiuna."*
Stranger: *"I've never heard of it."*
Me: *"It's a city, located 40 km away from Blumenau."*
Stranger: *"Ahhhhhhh yes! It's a first-rate city. But once you shift to second gear, the city disappears."*

Throughout my entire childhood, I heard the same joke.

Some people from small towns get defensive with such comments, and sometimes passersby can be particularly insensitive ("Do you drive a tractor?" "You don't look like you're from a small town!" "Your homes are so adorable!" ...) Personally, I took zero offence. In fact, I thought it made sense to describe the city that way.

Apiuna *is* a very small city; it's a municipality in the Brazilian state of Santa Catarina and it's just 3km wide. I'd describe it in a similar manner: *"You know when you're driving on the highway, and you see plenty of trees or nothing around you? And then out of nowhere, you see some houses, a church, a city hall, and you're back to seeing absolutely nothing around you? That's Apiuna you just passed through! You'll pass us in the middle of the highway. We've got two paved streets on each side, and the rest of it is dirt roads. It's 8,000 people in total".*

Apiuna is where I learnt that if I worked hard, I could have anything in the world. If I worked hard, I could be worthy of money, and I could be worthy of love. My childhood in the small city taught me that while work was necessary for anything I wanted in life, with work, anything was possible.

Apiuna was where I was born, where I'm originally from, and where I grew up until I was 17. My childhood in Apiuna had a *lot* to do with work.

The city's supermarket, the "Supermercado Fistarol," was my father's family supermarket, and it was very dear to him. He grew up there, caring for the business deeply, and still works there at the age of 75. It rubbed off on the rest of the family.

As a child in Apiuna, I also had my mother, who passed away a few years ago. She was strong, caring, and entrepreneurial: she worked in the supermarket, took care of the church, gave communion courses, led the mum's club, organised events for the rotary club, sewed and knitted, hosted and looked after several homeless people, *and* raised me and my two siblings.

From what I've heard, she loved to explore new places and travelled Brazil before she met and fell in love with my dad. (He was from the city - the pavement street, and she was from the farm - the dirt street). She married him and had a family.

Even before I was born, my mum would tell everyone: "My kids - I will allow them to go anywhere they want. If they want to go to China, they will go to China."

There was no way for either of us to have known back then that I would make it not only to China, but also to the USA, Canada, Australia, Thailand, Dubai, Hong Kong, Vietnam, Macau, Ethiopia, Indonesia, Spain, Portugal, Philippines, Malaysia, South Africa, India, Singapore, Taiwan, Japan, South Korea, Myanmar, Cyprus, the UK, Italy, Germany, Bulgaria, Colombia, Mexico ... the list goes on and on. There was no way we would have known that I would study, work, travel, love, live and thrive in the most far-flung corners of the world.

What I *did* know even back then was that I would leave Brazil. I had nothing supporting my desire to leave: no money, no education, no contacts abroad, nothing. And yet, I was certain I would leave.

You need to believe in the *what*, way before you know the *how*.

I knew that I would make it – and I did.

◆ ◆ ◆

DIARY ENTRY 2

All the World's a Stage ... (And All of Us Have a Part to Play)

The thing about small towns is that they deeply impress upon you a whole range of contradictory human emotions.

There's a sense of harmony and balance in everything, and at the same time, you also derive a serious work ethic. You're loyal to where you're from, but your heart yearns with longing for more. You grow up loved and supported by a tight-knit community, but also need to be extremely responsible. There's a comforting familiarity, but also a raging drive to be independent. There's usually a shared sense of purpose, but everyone's got to play their individual indispensable part.

For me personally, perhaps the most important quality I absorbed from my childhood was a sense of ownership. I could see how every person's contribution really mattered in the larger scheme of things, no matter how big or small the task.

My dad and mum were very different in their dispositions, but what they had in common was a crazy work ethic: I was able to see, from both of them, the importance of hard work.

From my dad, I learnt a lot of things just from observation and experience. With his supermarket, he worked nonstop, from 7:30 am to noon, and then again from 1:30 pm to 7:00 pm, with a short lunch nap at home in between. But he always radiated good vibes. He'd make time for us: he'd come home, we would have dinner together, and watch TV. He'd find ways to encourage us to study, work hard, and congratulate us when we performed well. I looked forward to Sundays the most because it would be the day my dad would be home and give his full attention to us. We would play soccer, wash his old car (a Belina), or go with him and the neighbourhood kids to the playground in the other city.

But before we got to play with him or help him on Sundays, we had to finish our weekly chores. The weeks would usually feel ordinary: I helped my mum and siblings with house tasks when I wasn't studying. I would usually dry the clothes or the dishes, and my mum insisted on the work being done correctly and completely. I remember vividly not finishing my chores one week. That Sunday was a "wash the Belina" one, but I didn't get to help Dad with it because I hadn't finished my housework. This memory stuck, because it reinforced in my mind the connexion between working hard, finishing what you're responsible for, and being worthy of opportunity.

My mother's nature was different from my father's, and while in hindsight I learnt a lot from it, back then it was certainly difficult some days. For example, I remember making 6 girlfriends at this new college in the nearest city called Ascurra, but I never invited them home because I was scared that my mum would put them to work! I also remember her once telling me that with the stress she has with me and the money she spends, she could have gotten another helper/cleaner for the house – can you imagine how painful it was to hear my mum saying that she would rather have another cleaner than me as her daughter?

But she was in a bad temper with everyone. Even my dad. When I was about 10, I even asked my dad if he ever thought of leaving my mum, and he said, like he always did, that we didn't see the "real" her, that she was soft and sweet inside, and that he would always know how to melt her heart. I remember how he loved her, unconditionally, for her entire life, while she would often scream at him, call him lazy or tell him he'd done everything wrong.

What Dad said about Mum would be true, sometimes.

I have memories of her surprising me. I was 13, and it was my birthday, but we didn't really expect parties back then. After school one day, she asked me to deliver something for her, and I remember walking down the street, feeling blue because I thought no one would wish me a happy birthday. When I got back home, all my girlfriends were there, waiting to surprise me! My mum hosted a beautiful little party, and laid out a delightful table; everyone was happy, mum was happy, and she was nice to everybody. I remember feeling thrilled. She was always terribly nice whenever we were sick, and supportive with little things like when you needed to use the washroom and you were outdoors.

In hindsight, it is only now that I can understand a lot of her behaviours and reactions. She'd be ill-humoured and would scream at us for not getting our tasks done, but I realise now that she was actually in pain herself, with a lot of unprocessed traumas within her. I wish I could have sensed this before and given her more love.

But for her part, she worked a tonne, just like Dad, and perhaps even more. And since it was made clear that we needed also to help, we grew up accepting our roles as contributors to our little world and we worked a tonne as well.

I suppose no matter who you are, what stage of life you're in, or what you do, if you look closely enough, you will find that you have a part to play in the larger scheme of things.

The more you own your part, and the more you build a mindset of contribution, the faster you can grow.

◆ ◆ ◆

DIARY ENTRY 3

It's about the Work, Not the Role

I think most teenagers, especially those from small cities, feel like caterpillars inside their cocoons, and can't wait to become butterflies. It was certainly like that for me.

My years in Apiuna were over soon enough. I was 18, and it was time to graduate and go to university. I'd played this event over and over in my mind, feeling the pulsating excitement of getting out of Apiuna, leaving my parents' house, and starting to live on my own.

Do you remember the rush of emotions you felt when you had to leave for university?

It's scary to leave the sanctuary you've known your whole life, and exhilarating to enter the vast unknown ... the colourful images of new adventures, the fear of fitting in, the excitement of finding yourself, the rush of endless possibility ... there's nothing quite like it.

The safety net of the hometown behind me, off I went, wide-eyed with the allure of discovery and independence, to discover my life's path. I went to live in the magnificent island city of Florianópolis, the capital of Santa Catarina, Brazil.

My family at that time were not in a strong financial situation, but my father, as I mentioned earlier, prioritised education. He had always agreed to invest in our studies; to him, our education would be the legacy he left for us. But as we would soon discover, after my first year in university, the expense of my tuition plus my house plus my meals plus my parties were adding up and becoming too much for him to take on, and so he told me that if I did not get a job, I would return to Apiuna. (I could study what I was studying in a closer city called Blumenau as well, with a free bus for the commute, but I didn't want to study there: I wanted to live by myself).

I did what most people in the same circumstances would do – I got a job.

There was an opening for an assistant for an events producer, so I went to an interview. The company owner said he could not hire me because I had no experience, but that he had an opening for a receptionist/secretary position, which paid even more, and which I was suited for. I never really understood how a secretary could earn more than a production assistant, but what the hell? I took the job.

Years later I would discover that he only hired me because he found me pretty, and that there wasn't even a position open. It didn't matter: as far as I was concerned, it was a win-win. I got to study and stay in Florianopolis, and he got the best secretary he could ever dream of.

If anything, he got the better deal.

I would go on in life to hold many positions of authority in the corporate world, but even back then, in that first serious role, I deeply cared about the work I delivered and the impact I made. That is what drove me, more than what my title was on paper (or being hired for being pretty).

Soon enough, my work began to speak for itself.

The first task given to me was to organise the events files. Jeffrey Ricci was a big name in the show business industry: if there was a show happening in the city, it would be him organising it. They gave me about 100 boxes and some 500 event files to organise, in a way that they could be found easily for any event.

I LOVED the work, and I absolutely killed it. They had just been wanting to keep me occupied, but they had no idea what I was really doing, and when I was done, everything was organised so well that I could find what anyone asked me to find – across hundreds of files – in a matter of seconds!

Jeffrey would take me to every single meeting to organise the minutes, and I loved attending those meetings. I'd pay attention, understand the issues, and record the promotion strategies. Minutes would be ready within 30 minutes and would blow everyone's minds, while I'd learnt a tonne. In two years, I'd not only be helping with event promotion, but also with production. I was truly happy organising things and making people's lives easier.

It was my actions, my passion that counted. I had a genuine desire to make a positive contribution (and not everyone does). I cared more about the quality of my work, the relationships I built, how much I learnt on the job, and how creative and skilful I was becoming.

People seek out fancy roles, but to me, it was always about the work, not the role. I'd do the work, and doors would open. I was learning more in life than in the university.

◆ ◆ ◆

DIARY ENTRY 4

Live Your Dreams and Pay Your Dues

In the university corridors where I studied Communications, in Florianópolis (and I'm sure, in many cities around the world), there's an ongoing, infectious buzz about "work experience in the USA".

Our school had a programme during the university break - between December and March. Those who went for the programme would return with fascinating stories of life in the Land of Opportunity - how fun it was, how much money they made, and the never-ending adventures they had. Hearing this would leave a burning desire within me to go live this dream for myself. In the second year, I started asking my father for money, and he would always deny me, simply because he didn't have it. I'd insist, having learnt from others that I'd be able to repay him whatever he paid, because I'd be able to work and earn in America. After two years of persuasion, he agreed in my fourth year, on the condition that I would pay him back.

Great! There was just one problem now: I didn't know any English.

But I'd figure something out!

There were two ways for me to go about the opportunity. The first was by being employed, usually by a resort; representatives would interview you and, if you were approved, you would have a paid job plus a place to stay. This didn't work for me because I could not communicate at all and convinced nobody to hire me. The second option was to go independently and find a job while in the USA. The problem with that, would be the extra cost for living. Luckily for me, my boss, Jeffrey, hooked me up with a friend of his: a Brazilian lady who had married an American and would be grateful to have someone living in her house to maintain it well and keep it clean. The deal was I'd clean her house, and gain accommodation in exchange, while I could go about and find a job that paid me. Worked for me!

I left for America, my head dizzy with dreams I wanted to live out, and mindful of the money I'd have to figure out a way to earn.

If you ask me today what that stint was like, I will tell you it was terribly difficult and deeply inspiring at the same time.

It is not always easy to pursue a dream, big or small, and you can never entirely foresee what it will take to make it come true. But if you find a way to take the leap - or even just to take that first step - you'll find you're able to see the next step, and then the next, and the next, and soon, you've lived out your dream, and have a heart and head full of experiences to remember.

It was 2004, and I was 20 years old when I landed in the USA. Mariana's home was the typical American house, spread over two floors and a basement - it was huge, and I was glad to have my own room in the basement. At the time, I couldn't want anything more. I just had to keep the house clean, I'd mostly work when she wasn't home, and make sure her dog hadn't left any droppings lying around. She travelled a lot for work and left behind a van for me to use if I wanted to.

My work for Mariana might have been simple, but what I took away from her was invaluable. Seeing Mariana travel so much, even getting paid to travel to a new country every week lit a fire within me.

Though I can't pinpoint it, maybe seeing Mariana's life was what began within me that insatiable desire for adventure across the vast tapestry of the world. Just watching her travelling non-stop felt intoxicating – imagine that sense of wanderlust and curiosity we all have, actually being lived out! The anticipation of setting foot on foreign soil, over and over, while growing professionally in life ... the connexion with people from all corners of the world ... the thrilling rush of the new, followed by a deep sense of fulfilment ... it felt like a dream.

I had my driver's licence, so I'd grab maps and directions from the internet (we had no Google Maps or GPS navigation back then, which was great because it forced me to speak to others in English). I'd take the car and just drive, feeling happy, adventurous, and courageous. I'd go meet people or go to parties.

I hadn't forgotten the money I had to make, and I ended up making money in three different ways.

A friend had told me to look for windows that said, "Now Hiring," and after a week of knocking on doors, I had received and accepted two job offers. One was at Wendy's and the other at a Bob Evans, neither of which required me to speak English.

Working at Wendy's (which is just like McDonald's) was fun. I fried potatoes. After a month, I was "promoted" and started taking orders at the cashier. My bosses were Indian, and my colleagues were Mexican; I definitely picked up more Spanish than English at Wendy's.

The Bob Evans stint was hard manual labour. I cleaned tables, floors, and washrooms. I cried more than once of exhaustion, hiding myself inside the washroom. It also turned out to be truly humiliating, but I kept my head up and just worked. A lady customer once asked me for more butter, speaking in English, which I didn't understand. I signalled to her that I'd go get the waitress, but she stood up in the middle of the restaurant and complained loudly. I later understood what she had said, which was along the lines of, *"You come to my country to work, you don't even speak English, what are you doing here?"*

I still wasn't making enough money, so Mariana helped me by fixing me up to clean her friends' houses. It was so strange - if I was cleaning for Americans, they would love my work, but if I was cleaning for Brazilians, they would always complain.

Anyway, I did the best I could. And while it was back-breaking work, I choose to remember the positives: I saw how America works, marvelled at the highways, explored new places, saw snow for the first time, and even learnt a little English. Oh, and I gained 10kgs eating all those burgers. Once I had enough to repay my dues, it was time to leave and return to Brazil.

I remember hoping that my dad would refuse to take the money because he knew how hard I had worked for it, but he took it anyway, and that was that.

I promise you, it was really hard – chasing my American dream while being mindful of my responsibilities. But that was the way I was raised – the same lesson sunk into me, deeper and clearer this time: Work hard for your money and pay your dues.

Dad got the money and I returned to Florianópolis to continue working for Jeffrey.

◆ ◆ ◆

DIARY ENTRY 5

There's *Always* Room for Negotiation

Sometimes we learn the most important things without anyone consciously teaching them to us. We just have to be paying attention, hungry to learn, and eager to grow.

Most of you who've been a part of the corporate world will relate to the following conversation with my boss, Jeffrey, who I was working for again after my USA stint. We were negotiating in R$ – Brazilian Reais.

Me: *Jeff, the sound system is costing R$10K.*
Jeff: *What? No, we don't have the money. You need to get this for R$7K.*
Me: *But I have quotes from three different companies, and the lowest is R$10K. How can I get it for R$7K?*
Jeff: *I don't care. Get it for R$7K.*

Sound familiar?

I was stuck; we had to make a certain tour happen, and I had to play my part in organising the event.

When something like this would happen, I would go back and call the companies, super embarrassed, telling them about my limited budget. They would negotiate, no doubt, but they had a peculiar pattern: they would always come back to me with a number that was mid-way between their asking price and my budget price. So, in this case, if the original quote was R$10K, and I asked them to make it work at R$7K, they would come back to me with an offer of R$8.5K.

Noticing the pattern, I began to quote an even lower budget price from my end. Soon enough, I was able to get prices that were better than what my boss had asked me to close at.

While it wasn't obvious, I'm sure Jeff knew he was teaching me how to negotiate, and I'm grateful for the lesson to this day.

The next time you're in a similar spot, do what I did. Check the market price of the item of your interest, then ask the seller for a 40% to 50% discount, so that you can eventually close at a minimum 30% discount.

You can even use my exact, fail-proof speech for reference:

"I *really* like your company, and I resonate with it above all others. Unfortunately, I don't have that much of a budget. It's my boss's fault; he will insist I go with the cheaper option. But I know, down to my core, that you're the best, and I really want to work with you! Could you possibly arrive a price that's closer to my budget? Then I can go talk to him on your behalf ..."

It works.

There's one more way to go about this. Instead of trying to lower the price, ask for more products or more services at the end of your bargain. For example, I once had to negotiate the purchase of 100 bags, and the price wasn't being lowered. I ended up asking for a reduced quantity – 95 bags and subsequently asked for 5 extra bags thrown in for free. It worked – it was just a matter of positioning the numbers differently.

In my experience, one of the two above techniques always works. There hasn't been a single time I haven't gotten my target price.

Don't ever be afraid to negotiate – there's *always* wiggle room.

◆ ◆ ◆

DIARY ENTRY 6

Show First, Ask Later

Luckily for me, since the early stages of my life, I've known how to ask for my worth.

I want the same for you – I want you to know your worth, and I want you to know how to ask for it. There are many different ways of doing this.

In my work with Jeffrey, over a two-year span I had already jumped 200% in salary. When I returned to Brazil, I was hired again to be an assistant for higher pay. Jeff was well-known to be a tight-fisted boss (as many bosses are!). And this wasn't just with external vendors, it was also with employees, which included me. For my part, I worked incredibly hard and got results. I did more work than was expected of me. I ended up producing a music tour all by myself. I did the work first – I made everybody love me. Six months down the line, I knew I deserved better pay, and I wanted another raise – but he wouldn't budge, and it appeared as though I had reached a threshold with him.

It so happened that I was loving the "events" life; I wanted to study it formally, and to have a post-graduate degree in the field. It was then that I thought of another way to approach Jeff.

Sure, it would have been great to get a raise, but it was even better to get knowledge. Knowledge is your power, and no one can take it from you.

So instead of asking him for a raise, I figured I could ask him to pay for my studies! After all, both he and I would benefit if I went out and learnt more about the events industry.

My plan worked, and I succeeded in getting him to sponsor my post-graduate education.

The lesson is here simple: Know your worth. Then prove it – first show what you can do for others. After that, ask to be paid for your worth, in a way that is palatable to them. When you've done the "show" part, the "ask" part becomes easier, and the ask can be anything: cash or another kind of investment in yourself.

If you're struggling to ask for a raise, consider asking for an investment in your upskilling, talent development, or education. How can you push your own growth further, in a way that also benefits the company you work for? Figure this out and go ask for it: not only will they like your suggestion, but they'll also happily make the investment.

◆ ◆ ◆

DIARY ENTRY 7

Finding Love (and Keeping It)

Is any book of adventures complete without love - its joys, and its loss?

Leonardo was everything I could ask for. He was handsome, caring, and excellent company. I met him in the strangest of ways. A month after returning to Brazil, at a nightclub, I was approached by someone who said, "I have a cousin, he is in London right now, but he is coming back to Brazil. He will find you very attractive. Can I get your email and give it to him?"

That was new for me but I remember saying, "Oh well ... why not?"

Everything moved very quickly, as it sometimes does in relationships – a wonderful combination of lucky coincidences.

We exchanged a few introductory emails, and lost touch. After 3 months, we just happened to bump into each other at a beach, where we talked for a bit, and again lost touch. A month later, he happened to be invited to my graduation party by a colleague of mine – and that night was our first kiss. No more coincidences were needed after that.

We went to the beach after the party, talked until morning, and started dating – after 3 months (and some drama), we were officially a couple.

Everything was great! What I most admired in him was his travel experience. He had lived in London for two years, visited France. And he spoke English. At the time, that got me fascinated. He was very supportive of me too – he'd pick me up the several nights that I would fly in late after organising events and he took me travelling to Argentina and Uruguay.

But do you know how it is when you have a driving force within, telling you clearly you need to do something – almost like a calling? For me, that was travel abroad. I couldn't wait to travel again and again - and Australia was my dream. I would tell Leonardo, but I confess I'd feel like this was always a cloud in our relationship, because he wanted things to go differently. He wanted to get engaged, while I mainly, above all else, wanted to travel overseas.

Sometimes things connect in ways we can't foresee. We cannot know how something will work out, but perhaps our job is to know exactly what it is we want and believe that it will work out.

In 2007, Brazil went through an incredible economic growth spurt. The guy who took care of finances for Jeff had taught me to invest in IPOs. It's important not just to get good advice, but also to act on it – and I had. By 2008, I had enough money to pay for my travel to Australia, and I decided to go.

I promised Leonardo I would return after 6 months, and we decided to continue our relationship. I was going to do both: keep the love I had found and pursue my calling to travel to faraway lands.

◆ ◆ ◆

DIARY ENTRY 8

The Land Down Under

Do you know that feeling of crazy excitement and anxiety of travelling abroad, solo?

You're at the airport, doubtful about finding your flights. It's about to be your turn to talk to the immigration officer, and you're wondering, "What will they ask me?" or "Will I know how to answer the questions?" and "What if something else comes up?" or "Will they let me in?" Of course, you have your paperwork in your hands ... where you're going, where you will stay, the funds you have, your donor's bank accounts ... your visa is stamped on your passport ... everything you can think of is ready, but that rush and the nervousness just doesn't subside. "I can't mess this up ..." is all you can think, because that's how badly you want it.

What is it that makes solo international travel such an addictive, incomparable experience? Perhaps it's because amidst that cocktail of emotions - adventure and doubt, confidence and uncertainty, independence and insecurity - there is a chance for self-discovery and true growth that very few other pathways in life can provide.

If you ever get the chance to travel solo, whether you're a young executive at a large organisation or a student wondering about your career, I advise you to take it.

Your window to the world will expand, as your mind stretches open wide. You will network and build meaningful connexions with people you could have never imagined meeting. You'll become more empathetic, and surer of yourself, both at the same time. You will be forced to communicate with people from different geographies and backgrounds, and you will learn SO much. You'll learn how to solve problems. You'll learn how to adapt to situations. You'll learn how to lose yourself in a magical new experience or custom, and you'll unlock a whole new dimension of yourself. You'll get to know your own strengths and your own weaknesses. You'll become more resilient, more independent, more confident, more skilful. Need I convince you further?

It's natural to be nervous, but it helps to sort out, in advance, the small things that are in your control. In this instance, to feel more comfortable, I got myself a car to pick me up at the airport and take me to my homestay. The car that showed up was the limousine kind - which felt great, because I felt like a princess off to my new adventure.

I will never forget the feeling of driving into the house – this massive, gorgeous house in Vaucluse Bay, on a cliff, overlooking the Tasman Sea. I will never forget meeting Vick and Ruth, the old couple that was receiving girls like me to stay at their home for the past 20 years. I would be staying there for a month.

Australia – my dream – and I was there!

◆ ◆ ◆

DIARY ENTRY 9

Gig Work and English Lessons

Do you ever wonder why is it so important to know English?

It isn't just that being able to communicate effectively can land you a good job and translate to career success, although that is the main advantage. I think knowing English does so much more for people from all parts of the world. For one, it keeps you from being insulted (as I felt in the incident with the lady at the American restaurant). Next, it helps you build personal connexions with people from far-off cultures. It helps you expand your knowledge. It helps you walk through new territories much more easily. It makes you feel empowered, and like you belong.

You may find something in your own life that makes you feel like it will open up the whole world to you – a language, a skill, a talent. When you're lucky enough to find this, you should chase it with your whole heart.

And so, I went to Sydney to study English, at a school called Selc. I remember very well that my choice of school was based on how many Brazilians would be there. I wanted there to be as few as possible, to force myself to learn more English. I even paid more because I was promised not many Brazilians would be there. When I got there, at minimum 50% of the school was made up of Brazilians. I started from the beginners' level; communicating with Asian people at a beginner's English level is no easy task, but I was determined to learn proper English. So I'd hang out with the Japanese and Korean and Thai crowd.

For similar reasons, I wanted to find a place to live where I would be surrounded by native English speakers, and I eventually ended up in an apartment in downtown Sydney with several others: two guys from New Zealand, one from Poland and one from Australia. My roommate was from Colombia. The Australian had different priorities, but the rest of us got along superbly, and the following 5 months turned out to be one of the best periods of my life.

We'd cook together, club together, go to the park, explore the city, laughing and playing all day long, and even when I couldn't follow the conversations closely all the time, I truly loved being amidst people speaking English nonstop.

There's that saying – you become like the 5 people you spent most of your time with; this environment was helping me, and I felt like I was thriving.

As my English got better, so did my work options.

I managed to get an amazing, well-paid gig at Cirque du Soleil, selling popcorn and making good friends.

I also took on the role of "freelance waitress," working for two different agencies that would ring me to waitress when an event happened, which would normally be a wedding. This gig was also easy and fun: holding a heavy tray of drinks, looking after 3-4 tables, serving food, removing plates, cleaning up, and repeating the process. The time would fly. I had my own waitress uniform, black pens, white shirt, black tie and black vest, a tray and a bottle opener. I was proud to be a functions waitress; it was a sought-after gig amongst us students, and the money I made was enough to pay my bills for the most part (and whenever there was a dip in cashflow, I'd go collect coins to buy a McDonald's burger to put something in my belly).

A side note here: there is a BIG difference between being a waitress in Australia and being one in the USA. In my first function, I was embarrassed to ask the guests what they wanted to drink because my English was still poor, but *every single person* was super receptive, spoke slowly, smiled, and explained well. In my first gig, I even spilled red wine on the long-sleeved white T-shirt of a guest; I apologised non-stop, but he simply said it was fine, rolled up his sleeves, actually smiled, and told me not to worry. Australians will always have my respect for the kindness and care they show everyone.

Overall, my life in Australia was magical.

In case you're wondering, I hadn't, of course, forgotten about Leonardo. I did have to ask him several times for some space to enjoy my experience of the new country, and he was respectful and understanding. (I don't know if he was seeing somebody else at the time, but the thing is, I honestly did not care, because I was living my life fully).

But I will confess, those 6 months were over in the blink of an eye, and I did NOT want to go back to Brazil. I expressed this to Leonardo and told him I was planning to stay longer, but he reminded me of my promise to return.

Perhaps it's not wrong to prioritise the aspect of your life that you're loving over every other aspect, but personally, my integrity, my word, means the world to me, and I am proud to keep it. I did not want to break my word.

At the time, I thought, all right - if I was going to go back, I would make the most of the time I had. With my savings and some financial help from Leonardo, I paid for an Australia adventure for 15 days, to be followed by backpacking around Thailand and Dubai on my way back, for another 15 days. Total 30 days before returning to Brazil.

More adventure was calling.

◆ ◆ ◆

DIARY ENTRY 10

What Backpacking Really Teaches You

There are many things to take away from the backpacking life (thriftiness, creativity, adaptability, communication, spontaneity, independence, simplicity). But I think what it teaches you most is *gratitude*.

Have you ever had an out-of-body experience? When you kind of float out of your physical body and look at yourself from a different vantage point, like from the top, and you're just immensely grateful to be having that experience?

In the first 15 days, I had flown to Cairns from Sydney and was hopping around cities and beaches, making friends everywhere, understanding little, loving everything a lot, surrounded by different cultures – the Europeans, the Irish - my heart full. At night we'd sit around the fire telling stories, and I would think, *"Who would imagine, me, feeling safe, around a bunch of strangers, in the middle of nowhere in Australia, not understanding a word of what they say! THIS is adventure. Thank you, universe, thank you!"*

I think it's almost criminal, isn't it, to not do the things that make you feel so alive?

I hated that it would end – I hated even thinking about the end.

I had another 15 days: off to Thailand, my first ever Asian experience. The noise, the people, the food, the colours – everything was endlessly fascinating and super affordable. I saw Bangkok, Phuket and Phiphi Island. I landed in Dubai the day the Atlantis Hotel at the end of the Jumeirah Palm was being inaugurated; I saw those gorgeous fireworks from the Palm. The Burj Khalifa was still being built, but it was my dream to visit the Burj Al Arab, and I did manage to the next day. I paid to have breakfast inside the hotel. I was surrounded by columns plated in 24-karat gold, and the most gorgeous emeralds – it was surreal.

I had been a backpacker for 30 days, and loved every second of it, but everything must end, right?

I would soon be flying to Sao Paulo, and from there, to Florianopolis. At Sao Paulo, Leonardo was waiting for me with flowers. He'd organised a hotel, with the bed decorated with a heart of petals. It was so nice to see him, but I think I was just scared of how much he loved me, and how much I loved to travel. I hadn't missed him as much as he had missed me. Since the first minute I put my feet onto Brazilian soil, all I knew is that I wanted to go back.

I remembered in my heart my travels, and the gratitude I had felt for what were now memories.

Meanwhile, I kept my promise, and Leonardo and I started living together.

◆ ◆ ◆

DIARY ENTRY 11

5 Ways to Keep Hitting the Bull's Eye

On my return to Florianopolis, I could have gone back to work for Jeffrey again, but I wanted something more – I was ready to choose a more difficult path. I was clear in my goals, and true to myself. I had even returned with a target in mind: to get into the largest media group in South Brazil, the RCS Group.

The RCS Group had a presence in Rio Grande do Sul and Santa Catarina, with the former being the main base. The group had operations across TV channels, newspapers, online websites (the internet was just about to explode) and radio stations. It also had an events department. Every year, they organised an event called "Floripa Tem," a 2-month long festival around Florianopolis, which would include sport events, concerts, free tours, you name it.

My plan was simple. I would somehow get hired to help at this Floripa Tem, show my skills, and then be hired as events producer at the group in general. I knew the plan was bold, and that everyone in events wanted to work for RCS. Luckily for me, Leonardo knew a manager at the Group who got me an interview, which was really all I needed. The role would pay me almost nothing, but I didn't care, because I was after the opportunity.

I knew I would get the role – and that's exactly what happened.

I've found this to be true quite often; when you really *know* something, and you *believe* it will happen, it does. Our job sometimes is just to have courage, to listen to our intuition, and to trust that life will help us, and it will.

After getting the role, it was about setting one clear target after another, and hitting each target, again and again.

Here I was, at the beginning of my corporate journey, and I learnt at least 5 valuable things.

#1 - NEGOTIATION

You won't get very far in the corporate world without at least basic negotiation skills. Since I had worked at a very small agency with Jeffrey, each cent of expense had mattered. I had learnt how to correctly note and expense all important figures, and stay one step ahead of whoever was on the opposite side of the table. Negotiation was now in my bones – and it came in very handy. Everyone was extremely impressed with my spreadsheets and how well the figures were managed.

#2 - ORGANISATION

Once a week, there would be a full team meeting with all 20 of us, with each one having to present updates across check lists. I was surprised at how disorganised it all was, with only the manager having some reference paperwork. So I put my organisation skills to use; I asked everybody for their files, arranging them systematically, compiling the numbers, and helping the manager get a more holistic view of the event.

#3 - PROACTIVITY

I was already a rockstar when it came to smaller things like writing meeting minutes, and now everyone would know what was next on the agenda. I started gaining the trust of the team, as well as management (it really is important to gain *both*).

#4 - TEAMWORK

In general, my approach was that whenever I saw a way to help, I'd just help. At one point a flyer had a spelling mistake, and the events producer was waiting for a designer to come in to fix it. I knew a bit of Photoshop, so I did it myself for her (she could have done it herself too). You'll soon learn that people like to do very little outside of their expected scope of work, which can be great! It gives you more room to contribute, to set yourself apart.

#5 - SOLUTION-OBSESSION

Most people like to obsess over problems.

For instance, on the very first day of the event, we had 5 vans for visual communication circulating the city. One of these was stopped by a policeman (something about just 40% of the vehicle being allowed to be used for visual communication). In the office, people started looking for the logistics guy, and he was nowhere to be found. People started to discuss the problem in detail, who was responsible, how it could have been prevented, and so on. And I thought, why had nobody gone to the stuck van? I did not wait for a second longer - I took my car keys, went straight to where the van was, spoke to the policeman, apologised, explained the situation, and asked for 24 hours to fix the problem. I reasoned with him: there were a bunch of tourists waiting to be transported for the event, waiting for the van, and he let the van go. (The logistics guy would show up a few hours later, grateful).

That's how I was wired by then: if there is a problem, *there is a solution*. It doesn't matter whose problem it is – just do your best to help with the solution.

You don't need to have all the knowledge (I knew no more about logistics than my office colleagues). It's just the attitude that can make all the difference.

When it starts to get stormy, most of the time, you'll see a lot of loud voices, finger-pointing, blame games, and tears of frustration around you. Joining in this won't get you far, *but doing the opposite will*.

Take a step back, take a deep breath, and ask yourself: "What can I do right now, to tackle this head-on?"

Become obsessed with solutions, and challenges will start to look like opportunities rather than obstacles.

◆ ◆ ◆

DIARY ENTRY 12

No Pressure, No Diamond

Before I knew it, the Floripa Tem was over, and no fixed employment was available at RCS. The department told me they'll do their best to bring me in. In the meanwhile, to make some money, I started freelancing for other companies. In 3 or so months, I got a job offer to be an events producer at RCS Group. Boom! Goal achieved!

Trust yourself, and trust life. Remember?

I had not just gotten the role, I'd risen up the ranks much faster than I realised, and for all the right reasons.

The events team was small; it was just one coordinator and 3 producers.

The coordinator, Bruno was bold, tall, confident, and well-spoken. He was the type of person who'd have everyone's attention as soon as he walked into the room. But I had grown to be sceptical about this particular type of person, because in many cases they wouldn't follow through on the operations nearly as well as they delivered the sales pitch. You'll find a lot of people stay away from the pressure of the operations – and from actually getting their hands dirty.

I chose to be the opposite, and that's why Bruno and I made a very good team. I was never a good presenter, but a terrific operator. I'd come up with production ideas from my on-ground expertise, and he'd sell those to the directors. On many occasions he would pass off the ideas as his own: I chose not to care.

If you find yourself in a similar spot, I'd like you to do the same. Don't worry. Of course, it's nice to be recognised. But don't beat yourself up over lack of visibility or credit. Focus on your work, and don't just do the stuff you are hired to do and always look for opportunities to help others.

Time is your best friend, and if you just keep at it, you'll build your confidence, and time will show the world the reality.

Oh – and there's no room for your ego.

I won't pretend that you'll never feel angry or scared that you'll never get your due appreciation. It would really boil my blood that Bruno would turn to me and ask me to take notes about what needed to be done (when I was the one who had explained to him what needed to be done). He'd do this in front of the directors, to cement his authority and to feel important.

I learnt to keep cool. I knew that one day, somehow, the seniors would figure out who the actual mind behind it all was.

Trust yourself, and trust life. Remember? And I did.

I loved my work.

I loved the numbers, I loved the events, and I loved the tiny nuances of organising everything behind those events. And fortunately, I was really, really good at it all.

It helps to be fuelled by genuine passion *and* being really good at whole wide range of things. That combination will take you places, *fast*.

Everyone operated in silos and just cared about their own event, even if they were using the same supplier – say for promotional material. I noted patterns that could provide leverage to get better prices from vendors. I started a "campaign" of sorts to present to the team and our seniors how much we could save, and the negotiation power we could have, if everyone just communicated with each other. The same thing happened with events budgets. They were separated into categories, and it was very normal to allocate expenses into the wrong category if it had a higher budget, which made no sense to me (Why would I spend on flowers, and allocate the expense to the sound system?) The events coordinator didn't care. No one cared. But I did. I cleaned things up, and soon enough, I was the blue-eyed star of the group's finance department.

Even without events on the weekend, I was working Saturdays and Sundays, studying numbers, bringing in more organisation, and more foresight. In parallel, the demand for events and for our business was growing. Some nine months into my organising several events perfectly and being extremely involved in the finances, Bruno was fired. I don't remember why, only that it was connected to the mess around finances. Nine months, and I was promoted to events coordinator.

I had handled the pressure and shone through.

◆ ◆ ◆

DIARY ENTRY 13

Make It Look Easy-Peasy

The Journalist Congress (our version of, say, the Met Gala), was done once a year, and it was always in the State of Rio Grande Do Sul. So in 2010 when they decided to bring it to Santa Catarina, many were astonished.

Not only did the event come to Santa Catarina – the event came to me!

It was a BIG deal for me and for the higher-ups at the Group. The RCS Company president would attend – and he didn't attend many events. The directors needed to prove to their president that they could handle such an event. Everyone was in the spotlight. Everyone was under a lot of pressure. But I always worked very well under pressure, or rather, even better when I was under pressure. I didn't doubt myself for a second.

I knew a lot *could* go wrong, but also that nothing *would*.

I kept two things in mind throughout.

The first: When problems occurred (and they would), I'd use my energy to find solutions.

The second: Chin up, head up. I would trust myself, and my work, and not be pulled down by the opinions of others.

Organising a Congress event can be like living out a thriller, with a couple of climaxes, anti-climaxes, and hopefully, a happy ending. Let me walk you through one.

Part one is usually about creativity. It starts with coming up with a concept and finding a venue. This event was taking place in this state for the first time. We didn't have a massive stunning theatre, and we didn't have many venues that could fit 400+ people. I decided to propose the resort Costao do Santinho as the venue, called my suppliers of Audio and Visual, and ask them to get *really* creative. They came up with the idea of a massive, curved screen that would take up the entire stage, using something called "multi-projection." Obviously, it was important to get the projection right for everything - the graphs, the videos, the passages - and so we hired the best visual artist in town. If you need to unleash people's innate creativity, next time, try asking them: *"What have you never done before, but know is possible?"*

Next comes part two: communication. We had to plan the orientation for the participants, many of whom would come from other cities. I came up with a welcome letter, an agenda announcement, a mini-map to help them localise themselves, and effective ways to deal with multiple, simultaneous check-ins at the hotel.

Part three is approval from the higher authorities, in this case, the Executive Director of the group. I had been around him many times, but never had a meeting with him. He was worried about the confirmation of the attendees and the logistics. The work in itself was easy-peasy for me, and I had everything in my spreadsheet: how many invited, how many confirmed, where they were coming from, what transport they needed ... but I didn't have it organised in a way that I could give answers promptly. He started asking valid questions, and I would take 2–3 minutes to find the answer. This scared him, and he said, "I do not trust you. This event is extremely disorganised, and you will mess this up. In a week I want to have another meeting, and I want my answers, quick." This shook me up: sure, the executive director did not know me, and did not know I had things under control. But the next week, I was ready. All the information was compiled into a dashboard. Whatever question he had, the answer took seconds. At the end of the meeting he just said, "Better".

Part four is execution. It was go-time, and there's *always* a hiccup. One day before the event, we went to try out the curved screen, and it was shiny as hell – so the projection was not visible! The wrong canvas had been used. I had a little breakdown, but someone had the idea of pressing matt ink on top of the shiny canvas, and I thank the gods it worked! We were almost good to go. At the last second, the Master of Ceremonies, a famous journalist from a night TV show arrived. She showed her disgust at the set, I remember her saying it looked super poor and she was ashamed to have the event happening there. Well ... she was wrong!

The event went on, and there was not one person that was not impressed by the massive curved screen, the efficient transportation, the easy check-ins, the clarity of the agenda, the comfortable chairs, and about ten thousand other things that had been managed down to a T, gracefully, passionately, and made to look so easy. The event was a roaring success.

The president of the group wanted to know who organised it, and one of the directors introduced us. Bruno may have gotten his visibility with the managers and directors, but Luciana was now known by the president.

◆ ◆ ◆

DIARY ENTRY 14

Show, Don't Tell

I had made it to management, and I had just turned 24. A new role had been created just for me; I was the first ever events manager in the state of Santa Catarina. I got a 40% raise, but more importantly, company sponsorship for the MBA I wanted to do.

Meanwhile, the business model itself changed; with the boom in events, our in-house department was now going to be a separate, revenue-generating company by itself, standing on its own two feet. Before, I would answer to nobody and everybody at the same time, depending on the event. Now, I would answer to a specific director.

If I had felt like I was working a lot before, it was now about to get insane.

As a manager, it helps to have a clear sense of who you are and what your working style is going to be, so that you hire people on the same wavelength. Event production openings at RCS were highly sought after, so I'd get a tonne of applicants. But I was a hustler, and I wanted other hustlers on my team.

When it comes to work culture, everything is much more effective when people can *see* management styles (as opposed to being *told* what is expected of them).

For example, working weekends and 10-hour weekdays was my absolute normal, and everyone in the office could see this. I would purposely schedule interviews on weekends because events happen on weekends, and if an applicant wasn't willing to make it to an interview on a weekend, they would automatically be passed on. I'd confirm in my interviews that the applicants would have long hours – I would literally say: *"You will have no life. Is that what you want?"* I would only go ahead with recruitment if I got a genuine and resounding "Yes!" in return.

◆ ◆ ◆

DIARY ENTRY 15

Enter "The Fistarol"

As we became a proper company, I earned the nickname "The Fistarol".

Many were super scared to come talk to me; even employees reporting directly to me. But once they get to know me, I seemed to be able to earn their respect and admiration. I knew I came off strong, and boldly expressed my opinion. I didn't want to be the one who was easily scared, and I never hesitated to bring up my way of thinking, no matter who was in front of me.

The office had gotten a lot larger, but my team was cut, and only the strongest ones survived. I now had 5 employees, but depending on the demand, I could hire freelancers to help. At one point I remember we had some 50+ freelancers! It always depended on the size of the event and required me to bring in the absolute best of my managerial capabilities.

I *loved* management.

When you make it to the managerial ranks, and perhaps even earn your own nickname (The Iron Lady, The Godfather, The Wolf of Wall Street, the People's Princess, The King of Comedy ... whoever you're going to be), you get to define what kind of leader you are.

For my part, I decided to always discuss issues in private, and compliments in public.

We'd use a small meeting room near our office that was usually available (we called it the "whip room"). Every time one of my team members did something wrong, we'd step in there and discuss the problem. Every time we had something to celebrate, we'd do it loudly, with everyone.

It worked very, very well.

◆ ◆ ◆

DIARY ENTRY 16

What's a Perfect Life?

I loved my work. I was dedicated to it, as much as it is possible for anyone to be. I was grateful, from the bottom of my heart, for my growth, for my accomplishments, and for the journey that awaited me.

Meanwhile, by all accounts, my life with Leonardo was perfect.

But you know that feeling of, "it's not you, it's me"? Most people I know are on the receiving end of that phrase and that feeling. In my case, it was true the other way around - there was *nothing* wrong with Leonardo; it really *was* me. I kept feeling a storm gather inside of me, and kept wishing that it would quell. I continued with the relationship mainly because there was nothing else I could ask for in a man.

I was living in conflict with myself. Leonardo had asked me to marry him a year after I got back from Australia, I had freaked out, then said yes, and asked him to please wait another 2 years. The thought of travelling again was always with me. Leonardo knew, because year after year I would talk about it, even try to break up with him, saying I wanted to travel. And he would promise me we would do it together.

It was hard – not the relationship, but that turmoil within. There is a dimension of life that comes from a relationship, a comfort, a joy, that keeps pulling us toward it, to at least try to explore it, to keep making it work, to not give up on it. I wasn't the sort of person who would just bail. I was the sort of person who *didn't* bail.

On the outside, everything kept seeming fine. He was supportive of a work schedule that was truly insane and would drive most partners mad. He'd happily help with housework, and we'd find our balance. We'd spend weekends the way he liked – at Leonardo's cousins' house for a barbecue. I didn't love it there – everyone was really nice, but I didn't feel a connexion, and I didn't feel like I belonged. The deadline for us to start planning our wedding approached, but I still couldn't imagine myself in family life. I wanted to leave – to be free – but that wasn't a "real" reason to end a relationship ... or was it?

As I grappled with my thoughts, the turmoil within became overwhelming. I could have been thrown into multiple-event, work-related disasters or surrounded by terrible colleagues and it wouldn't have felt even a tiny bit as difficult as this. The love and connexion I had once craved (as every woman does), were now replaced by doubt and anxiety. The guilt of hurting a wonderful partner – the fear and pain of it – crushed my heart. Yet, deep down, my dreams called me.

Finally, I told him I needed to go on a short overseas trip, and I went to Canada for a bit. My sole intention was to think about my future, and to see if this mad thirst to travel could be quenched, once and for all. When I returned, there were no doubts in my mind: I needed to go live abroad again.

I would cry night after night after Leonardo slept. I did not want to make him suffer. I would pray that he would find another woman to love him and honour him as he deserved, as fast as possible.

He didn't deserve suffering. And I didn't deserve to live a life I didn't *really* want to live, a marriage I didn't *really* want to be in, all the while killing that inner clear love and desire of living overseas.

Finally, I decided to ask for professional help. I found a therapist, and after 2 or 3 sessions I felt more ready. I broke up with Leonardo. This time, there were no arguments, no excuses, no convincing one another. It was done.

We announced our breakup to both families after the holidays. My family were devastated; they absolutely adored Leonardo. His family were also sad to see their son sad, but I think at their core, they were probably a little happy (and rightfully so), because they always saw that I prioritised my work, and never him.

I remember the exact date - January 2nd, 2013 – that I went to Leonardo's apartment at a time he wouldn't be there, collected my belongings, and left. It had been 8 years that we were in a relationship! And it was all over.

◆ ◆ ◆

DIARY ENTRY 17

The Call of the Far East

I did not know yet where to go, or what to do. I had very little money, having spent most of it.

It didn't matter. Within me, I knew I would somehow figure everything out. I remembered how I had once made it all the way to Australia! I could do it again.

The first time doing *anything* big is the hardest, and also the most important, because the confidence it gives us stays with us for the rest of our lives.

I absolutely loved the sensation of being single, thinking and planning my life from scratch once again. On some level, the freedom didn't even seem real (yet). To make it more real, I wanted to inform RCS about my decision. I told my boss, asking him to be prepared for my departure at some point that year. He shared the information with his boss, who came down to try to talk me out of it, assuming I had not thought things through.

I knew what I was doing; I hadn't arrived at the decision of leaving a respected, coveted, well-paying corporate job on a whim.

I looked up to him, so I decided to open my heart. I told him of my desire to travel, to live every 6 months on a different continent. He had himself had a long stint abroad, so I figured he'd understand. Instead, he laughed and laughed, hard. He told me I was insane to think I could do it – that I would be working second-hand jobs, that it was silly to leave a high-salaried, managerial role to go be a waitress in foreign countries.

It often boils down to how badly you really want something.

What is louder: the voice within, or the voices around?

I wanted to leave, badly enough. And I wanted to listen to my inner voice.

Trust yourself. Trust life. Repeat.

Sometimes, you just need to open up your life to allow something new in – to make room for more than you can immediately foresee – to make way for magic. You won't always know how something will work out, and even then, you need to trust your end goal.

My end goal was to work overseas.

Looking at my old life, would being engaged and being employed full-time help me get closer to my end goal? The answer was no. I had needed to make those tough decisions to close certain doors, and I'd had the courage to do so.

I've seen this happen many times: Once you claim a true desire and start showing the universe you are serious about it and start taking aligned actions, rooted in a deep belief of what's to come, the universe will gift you with opportunities you never dreamt of.

I was brainstorming ideas over dinner with some girlfriends. Out of nowhere, one of them looked at me and asked, "Would you work in China?" and I went, "HELL YES, Clara, I would absolutely work in China, tell me more!"

She had literally had an idea at the dinner table; she was the product development director of the largest gift company in Brazil. Their development work happened in China. Communication between Brazil and China was always slow due to the time zones, and she figured it would be great for the company to have an asset based in China - someone who could communicate with suppliers, receive samples, and give back feedback to facilitate the process better. She knew I had been the events manager at RCS, and that the job had involved a tonne of negotiation. What neither of us knew was whether her company's CEO would be onboard. There was only one way to find out, right?

It took her a month to talk to her boss, who agreed to explore the idea and meet me.

Oh, interviews! I had never ever been denied a job after an interview, and I was extremely confident. I ended that meeting with an agreement to work for them 3 months based in Brazil, and then move to Hong Kong. The salary was going to be half of what I was getting at RCS, but I would have a paid-for house to live in. Was I happy with the offer? You bet!

In August 2013, at 29 years of age, I would be landing in Hong Kong.

◆ ◆ ◆

DIARY ENTRY 18

A Broken Full Heart

Pain is not always visible, and when you're dealing with a raw broken heart, it can be hard to feel anything good at all.

Then when you least expect it, something happens that makes joy and gratitude rush through your veins. You feel warm, from the inside out, at least for a little while.

I think this happens to everyone: there is always a ray of light to be found amidst a new darkness. Life does not take something away from us without giving us something (or many things!) in return. But we often don't see it or can't feel it. If we could, there would be much less sadness, anger and cynicism in the world.

So back to my story – the Far East was calling me! And I, the big and scary "Fistarol" had announced to my team members that I was leaving. On my last day of work, one of them said they needed to talk to me in the "whip room." I got there, expecting some trouble, but my whole team was there with a cake and a sign that had some

Chinese writing on it (the meaning of which remains unknown to me to this day), to wish me goodbye. I had given my sweat, blood, and tears to my work for many years, but I hadn't expected the love and appreciation I got from my team, and it meant the world to me.

I would go on to have countless other journeys and meet several other colleagues, but I remain extremely grateful for each one of those teammates to this day.

As I got ready to leave, many people in Brazil would come to me and say that they were very happy that I was going to Hong Kong and not China.

I honestly did not know the difference, but I was soon going to find out.

◆ ◆ ◆

DIARY ENTRY 19

Meeting the Superhumans

Truth be told, I was over the moon just to be going to work in Asia. Its exotic landscapes, ancestral wealth and practices of healing and rejuvenation, its rich heritage, its diversity, its rootedness mixed with its contrasts, its tech advancements, its hospitality ... and of course, its food! I honestly did not care whether it would be Hong Kong or somewhere else. To me, it was all uncharted waters.

But if you'd like to know the difference between China and Hong Kong, I'll tell you.

Hong Kong is pretty much its own country, with its own language, its own money, its own culture, its own business culture, its own passport. Its people are "Hong-Kongese," and not "Chinese." They're way more polite than the Chinese. They have more access to information and are much more integrated into the rest of the world. Hong Kong people are truer to their word, whereas the Chinese are more likely to be trying to find a way to take advantage of you.

I'll give you a handy tip: don't call Hong Kong people Chinese. While we're at it, just so that you don't ruffle any feathers, also don't call the Taiwanese Chinese, the Australians New Zealanders, the Indians Pakistani, the Koreans Japanese, or the Scottish English (and vice-versa) either! All these are wonderful peoples from their own lands with long (sometimes deeply messy) political histories, so why hurt someone you just met?

As for me – I had come to Asia looking for adventures, and I was going to get many more than I had signed up for!

I landed on Hong Kong soil, unable to contain my overwhelming sense of fascination, as my escapades began.

The first shock was my apartment, which I had been told would be "small but very well planned." I opened the door, and I was inside the kitchen. I walked two more steps, and I was inside the "room" – which was literally a bed sandwiched between walls. If I lay down on the bed, I could touch the TV across from it with my feet. Next to the sink in the kitchen was the bath, and what is apparently very common, was that I'd need to shower sitting in the sink (as there was no "shower area").

But hey, I was in Hong Kong! Who cared that the apartment was some 15 square meters?

What happened next, however, was something I *did* care about.

I went to sleep, and I felt something on my fingers, which I discovered were two cockroaches. A quick Google search told me cockroaches don't like light – so I turned the room lights on, pointed my iPhone light right onto my face, covered my eyes with a T-shirt, and went back to sleep. The next day I lay out traps for the little pests, and then went out into the city. On my return, I found at least 10 of them dead on my floor.

I was still trying to wrap my head around the miniature apartment, dead cockroaches, and new time zone, when my 10-day travels to visit suppliers around China began, with each new day leaving me in awe.

Every company we'd visit would receive us with a wreath of flowers, our names written in the middle. It felt absurd to me because we use the exact same flowers in Brazil, for funerals.

Seeing the factories and the actual manufacturing processes left me stunned. Up until then, whenever I had imagined factories, in my mind, the work would be done by machines. Here I'd see that it was humans doing it ALL.

Take picture frames for instance. I saw a production line with hundreds of people. One would grab the frame, another would put the glass, another would assemble it, another would put one screw, another the second screw, another would check, another would grab a box, and another would put it all inside the box ... it was crazy. And the mugs? I discovered that the handles of the mugs were glued on one by one. A person would be putting their hands inside the mug, dipping it inside a bucket with ink, being very careful to not allow the ink to go inside the mug, and taking it out (because the goal is to paint just the outside). This person would put the mug onto a tray which would take the mug into an oven to dry. Another person would be waiting at the end, to remove it, and yet another to transfer it into a box, and so on.

Every factory would have a "big boss," who usually would not speak English. The person who *would* speak English would be a generalist: a sales representative, general manager, and operations lead, all rolled into one.

If, during your factory visit, you needed to use the restroom, that would be a sensory overload experience by itself. The smell in the toilets of Chinese factories is something I won't even try to describe.

Oh, and the food! I loved the exotic delicacies (but definitely not the frog meat), hated the tofu, and drank lots of Baijiu (which is some 60%+ alcohol).

We went from city to city in China. The cities were either very small, loud, full of traffic, ugly, dirty, with a tonne of people spitting on the streets. Or, they were very big with massive buildings and large streets. Our last stop before heading back to Hong Kong was Shenzhen – and I remember looking out of the hotel room, seeing a tonne of lights, tall buildings, and well-dressed people, and thinking: "I could live here!"

Be careful what you wish for!

The universe would hear my thoughts, and I *would* live not only in Shenzhen, but in Futian, which was the exact neighbourhood of my choice. It so happened that during that China trip, my seniors and I realised how much more sense it made for me to live in China instead of Hong Kong in terms of legalities and logistics, and we decided I'd get an apartment via an agency.

◆ ◆ ◆

DIARY ENTRY 20

A Comedy of Errors aka Negotiation 101

The ordeal of settling into my new Shenzhen apartment was my introduction to negotiation in China.

I had instructed the agent carefully (no more cockroaches for me, please!). We had picked an apartment and a date and time for me to move in. I remember thinking it shouldn't be too hard – I just needed to rent a car service to get me and my stuff from across the border. I was outside the door, with all my clothes and work product samples waiting for the agent, when he said the move would happen the next day. I expressed my anger and insisted on him sorting out my entry on that day itself. He finally caved, and got me the key to put my stuff inside. I still had to sleep elsewhere that night, though.

With Chinese people, you need to show authority and if need be, literally engage in a fight to get them to listen to you. Don't back down.

The next day would be war, again, this time for internet connectivity.

My agent and I entered the internet service place, ready to haggle like champions. This seems to be the usual process in Chinese negotiations: they threw a price at us, and I exclaimed, "That's too expensive!" They said, "No discounts." I turned my back, ready to storm out in dramatic fashion, but as expected, as I reached for the doorknob, they called out, "Wait! We can offer you a better deal!"

But the dance had just begun.

Offers and counteroffers followed, and at long last, I thought we had a deal, when they dropped a bombshell: I had to pay an extra month because I had set foot in their establishment on September 30th, a day before the start of the next month. "Fine," I said, being a little tired by then, "I'll be back tomorrow." The next day arrived, and to my dismay, they had forgotten all about our previous deal. We found ourselves in a 30-minute replay of the same arguments, like déjà vu. Finally, we proceeded to sign the contract, and they dropped another bombshell: I had to pay an extra month because, apparently, hiring their services on the 1st of the month came with an absurd penalty. I let out a scream that must have scared onlookers. Thankfully, they settled and agreed to waive the "penalty" because I honestly could have done this no more.

My two biggest takeaways in negotiating with the Chinese?

Number one is: Be ready for battle.

Number two is: Have *patience.*

◆ ◆ ◆

DIARY ENTRY 21

Your Vibe Attracts Your Tribe

It was only after several months of settling into China and working non-stop that I realised I had no social life.

You can love your work, but that doesn't mean you shouldn't or can't have friends in foreign countries. If anything, you *need* to build a social life in order to remain motivated and supported at work. There's that old saying: no person is an island, and indeed, we aren't.

People think that I am an extrovert, but I am, in fact, a shy person. I deliberately go out of my way and choose to put myself in social situations because I know is necessary. I try to make it easier for myself by finding places where everyone's new, and everyone's come to make connexions.

And so, in what would turn out to be one of the best decisions of my life in China, I cancelled my meetings one night to go to an "International Networking Event" and meet a group of ex-pats I found on Facebook. (If you're looking to meet people in Hong

Kong, there's an App called "Meetup," but that didn't work for me in Shenzhen.)

I arrived at the event, got a free drink, a sticker with my name and my country's flag on it, and started walking around introducing myself. After about an hour I met Aden. Aden was from Israel and had been in China a few years. He told me about the best places to go to in the city, and about a series of upcoming events: Wednesday night live music here, Thursday night free margaritas there ... I'd go to these at night, catch up with him again, and meet his friends, who would start to become my friends as well.

It turned out that in no time, I knew a large group of spectacular people. As I went on to create a full social life, and grew more confident, I grew happier, and my work thrived as well.

As the days went by, my time in the far east turned out to be simply magical.

I guess I'm trying to tell you to get out of your comfort zone - I've personally never, ever regretted doing so.

◆ ◆ ◆

DIARY ENTRY 22

10 Lessons over Frog Meat and Baijiu

For your sake, I hope that someday you do business in China, or with the Chinese. And I hope you live in China, or with the Chinese.

When that day comes, I'd like you to remember these 10 things I learnt the hard way.

#1 - DRINK (BUT DON'T GET DRUNK)

In China, the basis for good business is good relationships.

The Chinese believe that you won't lie if you're drunk, which means that when you're drinking is the best time to talk business. I realised how crucial it was for me to have personally visited the factories and shown my face - it made all the difference in the collaborations that followed. To encourage you to drink, Chinese business associates will always, always bring Baijiu. You sit at the table, and it starts with everybody toasting together, after which the tradition is that the visitor toasts with every single person on the table - aka, they will each drink about 2 glasses, and you will drink about 15.

So get ready to drink a LOT (while somehow managing to not get drunk).

#2 - *MOVE*

No matter where you are in China, you'll see old people fill the parks, stretching in the mornings, or out on the streets, dancing at night. Old people in China are always moving their bodies and staying fit.

Why can't you and I do the same?

#3 - BE PATIENT

No matter how hard you try - Google and AI-assisted translation and all - there *will* be things lost in translation.

I was happy with my new home (the bathroom itself was bigger than my entire Hong Kong apartment), and I didn't want to lose it, so I went to the management office the very next day to pay my bills. They told me it was not necessary, I showed them in the contract that it was, and all I heard was "No." The next day, the lights stopped working (because I hadn't paid the bill!)

Then there were days I worked in a Dongguan factory, which we decided to open for the products we purchased most frequently in China.

I would take a train from Shenzhen to Dongguan, which was a city located an hour away. The public transport process in China is more or less the same: you go wait in line, the Chinese go in front of you, you tell them to not too, then they push you. You push back, do your angry face, finally get your ticket, get smashed between a zillion people walking to the train, finally get inside, and sit.

At the factory I'd meet Nancy, and all she would answer was, *"An"*.

Me: *"Nancy, this is a Yes or No question, Ok? Did you get the quote I asked for?"*
Nancy: *"An"*
Me: *"Yes or No, Nancy?"*
Nancy: *"An"*
Me: *"Do you understand what I am saying?"*
Nancy: *"An"*

That's China for you – it really does get challenging, so expect that in advance.

I'm sure I got several strands of white hair during my time there.

#4 – STAY ON TOP OF PRICE AND QUALITY

My work with Chinese suppliers was stressful, and my previous experience in negotiation (remember Jeffrey?) helped a great deal.

I applied the same technique here: when you are buying a new product, first get a quote from 4 or 5 vendors to have an idea of the price. Then ask for 50% off ... They will respond with 10% off. Then you say you'll go with another supplier because you *really* don't have the budget, and they will come after you a few days later, usually with a 40% discount and, in some cases, agreeing to your bid.

The other method is to play the MOQ (Minimum Order Quantity) game. If you wanted to buy, say, 3,000 units, you'd say you need

1,000, and with the negotiation underway you go, "Ok, what if I ordered 3,000 units instead?" You play along as though you're helping them, and they do the same as though they're helping you.

It is very, very important to note that sometimes they will accept your offer price, but change the product slightly. So if you're buying bags, for example, they might include a cheaper zipper or change the inner fabric lining. You've got to be extremely specific about the design and details you want in your agreement, and keep a close eye on the product materials.

#5 - LET THE LITTLE THINGS GO

The "unboxing" of the product was an experience in itself. Sometimes I would receive a sample the size of a pen, inside a box that could hold a 14" TV, with more empty boxes or lots of paper inside.

Insane! But you keep your eyes on the bigger picture.

#6 - FOCUS ON ABUNDANCE, NOT SCARCITY

I'll tell you another hard truth: China is not the easiest place to live for single ladies.

Picture this: you and a male friend are in a crowded bar, sitting close together so that you can hear each other over all the noise. Out of the blue comes a Chinese lady (who is usually very pretty), who gets in between the two of you (with her back facing you), and introduces herself to your friend. This isn't a one-off in China: single Chinese ladies can be very, very aggressive by the standards of other parts of the world, and especially when it comes to the pursuit of foreign boyfriends. I think a lot of it is to do with gaining status, and probably financial security (they assume these men have a lot of money, which in many cases can't be further from the truth). So if you're an expat guy from someplace abroad, your existence is enough for you to be bombarded with attention from several local ladies that want to be noticed by you (while leaving the foreign ladies a bit scared).

It isn't just about beauty, either. In my two years in China, I had a few quick romances in Hong Kong, but in mainland China, just one, very short-lived one. He later gave me some (terrible) advice, which was that to make myself more appealing and "gettable," I should lie and say I was something like an English teacher rather than a manager at an international company in charge of operations, finances, and expansion. For God's sake: how could lying about who I was (when I was really proud of it) be good dating advice?

I chose not to play this game. In such an abundant world, why believe in scarcity, of any kind?

#7 - KEEP CHECK OF YOUR EXPENSES

I was growing well at work, and visiting more and more supplier factories by myself (which I thought was amazing).

I was working during the days, with meetings at night, and eating at Western restaurants because I didn't yet have the courage to go to the real Chinese ones alone. I was also setting up the company operations in China, opening a bank account, finding an accountant, dealing with trademarks, and figuring out my visa.

It helped that in addition to all this, I surpassed all expectations with my expense reporting – I'd deliver these reports without being asked, and that made a massive difference to my reputation.

#8 - FOCUS ON THE LONG-TERM

It helps to promise your Chinese associates that if the product becomes a success, you intend to go back to them and buy a lot more.

The Chinese like to see they are embarking on a prosperous and long-term partnership.

#9 - OFFER MINDFUL HELP

You want to be helpful to your colleagues anywhere in the world, and not just in China.

In China, however, you're likely to come across colleagues who will change your definition of "workaholic," and who may feel very competitive. So you may have to be extra mindful of *how* you offer that help.

Take me and my colleague, Clara, and the episode of the Canton fair.

Clara was responsible for our product line. The Canton fair is the largest trade show in China, and Clara had attended these several times before and would continue to, now with me as her assistant (I still have my Canton fair badge - you get one for life!). Clara would have a very well-organised agenda. We would get to the fair by 8:00 am, to be at the door when it opened at 9:00 am. From 9:00 am to 6:00 pm we would walk around the fair nonstop. She knew the locations of the booths of all our suppliers and would manage to schedule meetings and dinners with them almost every night of the event, which meant we'd go to bed at 11:00 pm each night. It was exhausting. In comparison to Clara, I felt like a lazy arse - she was a machine!

She had her system which she asked me to copy entirely.

When she would find a booth with something she liked, she would take a picture of the product, and the business card of the supplier. She would ask for the factory location, Free on Board (FOB) price, and Minimum Order Quantity (MOQ). If the product was something that she was entirely sure she wanted to buy, she would spend a long time in the booth, already negotiating a better price and sometimes even making slight changes to the product. In total, this would be done for over 100 suppliers.

After doing this three times, I asked Clara what would happen with all this information after the fair. She told me she would just push it from her memory - she had the pictures on her phone, and the information in her notes. I could see here an opportunity for improvement - a way to help make the system more efficient. So I asked if we could put a number next to each supplier. Next, we marked as asterisk next to the suppliers she found of interest and was sure of partnering with.

After the fair, I organised all information from the business cards in a spreadsheet: supplier number, name, product of interest, factory location, price, MOQ, the pictures file number, and the asterisk mark. It made it SO much easier for us to communicate, and to find the information faster.

Luckily for me, Clara was receptive to my idea, even though she didn't trust it much. Later, however, she did thank me for the time it saved everyone, and we used that system for several other Canton fairs to come.

#10 - LEARN HOW TO ACCEPT HELP

In everyone's corporate journey, there comes a time when you need to team up with others. It's important to know how to accept the contributions of your colleagues gracefully, without feeling threatened.

It may sound great when you're told that you'll have an extra pair of hands but, in reality, it may feel challenging. And this is doubly true if you're in a competitive and fast-paced work environment where you've worked like crazy, building things from the ground up, only to have others come in and reap the benefits of what you have sown.

In March 2014, I received my first promotion in China. After that, I was not only doing product development work, but also managing company finances and setting up our own Chinese factory – the Dongguan factory – with Nancy's help. We agreed to hire a Brazilian to come work in China, who would assist me with sampling assessment and supplier negotiations (with some training from me). We chose Ana Wang: she was Brazilian with a Chinese background and spoke a bit of Chinese. We could not have asked for more! And yet, when she finally arrived and settled in, I confess I felt what was perhaps very close to jealousy. Wang would come in after all the hard work was done. The company was set up, the paperwork was ready, the physical location was established, and I'd made some wonderful friends ... all the hard way. Now, she'd come in and get all this on a silver platter. What made it worse is that she would be my roommate (I didn't even care for housemates).

It took me a while to get used to her, to learn how to trust her. I was, at first, awful to her. I was rude, demanding, and unfair. But she really *had* arrived just in time to help with the changes, and I couldn't have done without her. She was a strong woman herself. Bit by bit, we found our balance. In less than a month, she had melted my (unnecessarily frozen) heart, and we became not only healthy colleagues but true friends.

When you need help, and it is given to you, *take it*.

Accepting help won't subtract anything from your work or your life – it will only enrich both.

◆ ◆ ◆

DIARY ENTRY 23

It's a Wonderful Life

I had been journaling my thoughts and maintaining my notes, but after being in China for several months and living a rich, full, life, I decided to buy a beautiful diary to record my memories. I remembered an Englishman I had met in Vietnam who had made his own travel diary, and I loved the idea.

I found myself at the Hong Kong airport, waiting to go to Europe for the very first time - and my flight departed in 4 hours. I was thinking about my life in China. Just the previous night, I'd met some 30 amazing people at Aden's house party. I was living out one of the best times of my life.

Sure, the Chinese have an insane work ethic - but let me tell you, I am yet to encounter a country that has more holidays than China.

In May, there is Labor Day, a one-day holiday everywhere else in the world. In China, they celebrate it for a week. Across June-July there is the Dragon Festival, which means you get another 5 days off. In September, with the mid-autumn festival, another 3 days off. In October, with "National Day", you get another 10 days. And of course, there's the gala Chinese New Year which is officially 10 days with an additional (semi-official) week prior and week after for celebrations, which means it's really like having a month off. As if this wasn't enough, I got even more holidays because I was working for a Brazilian company in China, which meant I got all the Brazilian holidays as well: a 30-day vacation (that's the rule in Brazil: for every 365 days of work, you get a 30-day bonus vacation).

For the first time in my life, I found I had a tonne to do *outside* of work. I had friends to meet, fun activities to go to. Once a month there would be a psy-trance music party somewhere in a hidden part of the town (like in a tunnel or on top of a pagoda), organised especially for foreigners, which would turn out to be incredible.

And of course, I would use most of my holidays to explore the world.

I started enlisting my adventures into my new travel diary, and I think my explorations would have made even Marco Polo proud:

Diary entry
Name: *Luciana Fistarol*
Date: *24 August 2015*
Location: *Somewhere in China*

Today, it's been exactly two years since I left Brazil to come to the Far East, and I am so thankful for all experiences I have lived so far!

- *I camped on the Great Wall of China;*
- *I danced all night long in the streets of Hong Kong;*
- *I ate a lot (and got food poisoning) in Vietnam;*
- *I bungee-jumped, twice, dressed like Batgirl for one of them, and won a competition for the best jump in Macau;*

- *I washed my butt using my hands in Ethiopia;*
- *I got my first tattoo in Bali;*
- *I went topless dancing in Spain;*
- *I missed a flight and stayed back in Portugal for a few more days with no agenda;*
- *I swam with whale sharks in the Philippines;*
- *I spent all day with a Muslim client in Malaysia, chatting and learning about the wonderful Muslim culture;*
- *I touched lions in South Africa;*
- *I ate food with my bare hands in India;*
- *I spent a whole day in the swimming pool of a huge fancy hotel in Singapore, looking at the famous tourist attractions;*
- *I made wishes on a lantern in Taiwan;*
- *I had the best night out in Tokyo;*
- *I felt awestruck by the beauty and the white skin of the women in South Korea;*
- *I saw the sunset from the top of one of some 3,000 pagodas in Bagan, Myanmar ...*

◆ ◆ ◆

DIARY ENTRY 24

Paperwork and Passports

Do you ever wonder about your lineage, your family history?

When I was about 24 years old, I had come across my own origin story. It mattered to me at the time because it meant I could probably get a German passport, the pursuit of which would go on to take me on a mission that would last several years.

Here was my background: As a kid, my grandfather had come to Brazil from Germany, with my great-grandfather (he had learnt to walk while on the ship!) Under German law, this meant my mum was entitled to a German passport, and that she could pass the citizenship to her children (which meant I could have one). Relatives on my mum's side travelled a lot: they were wealthier, *and* they had German passports – and I wanted the same for myself.

I asked my mother why she had not got hers. It seems she had gotten scared off by the complications of the application process and assumed her children wouldn't need one. My mother had been an illegitimate child, which meant there was no proof of her being eligible for the passport. I was, however, able to deduce that proof of her lineage, tying her all the way back to my great-grandfather and grandfather, would be enough for the authorities. The paperwork I'd need in this type of process was the birth certificate, marriage certificate and death certificate of each member of her family: my mum, my grandfather, and my great-grandfather.

We had the documents until my grandfather, but as for my great-grandfather, all I had was his death certificate. I had to find out where he was born, and somehow get his birth and marriage certificates. After several years, I did find the papers and got the official copies all the way to Brazil, from a city that now was part of Poland (not Germany). At long last, with a little help from my sister (who initially annoyed me with several follow-ups without doing her part of the work), and from the German Embassy in Brazil, my mum's German passport was approved.

I heard this around the same time I had started thinking about leaving China for good. A perfect sign!

◆ ◆ ◆

DIARY ENTRY 25

Keep Your Head High

Meanwhile, a lot was happening in the company. Our CEO had joined with a new partner, Diego, who advised organisations for rapid growth. Diego was going to be the "Director of Process and People", and my new boss.

Alongside this, my deadline to complete my MBA (the one I had enrolled in, sponsored by the RCS Group) was approaching. Day by day, I could feel that the time was nearly up for my China stint.

Not one to leave people hanging in the balance, I spoke to my seniors and with Diego, who I had just met, informing everyone that I was planning to leave – which would mean I was giving 6 months' notice. To be perfectly honest, I didn't care much for Diego at all. He was very condescending, and our interactions would leave me feeling patronised and embarrassed after all I had done for the company. He had this way of talking down to people, and I hated that the "Director of *People*" wouldn't really hear his *people*. He would, for instance, at the end of a meeting look at me and say, "See, that's how you manage a meeting, and come in with smart questions ..." And I, who had managed to register two companies, open a factory, set up bank accounts, and register trademarks, all on the foreign soil of China, all by myself, would in my mind be thinking, "Really?! Are you suggesting I don't know how to do things, or ask questions?"

When you come across such colleagues (and I believe all of us do, at some point), it isn't always worth it to pick a battle. Sometimes, you just need to be patient - swallow hard, distract yourself, take a deep breath - whatever works for you, and just let the moment pass. And it isn't because the other person is right, or stronger, or has more authority - it's because *someone* has to take the high road. Conserve your energy for the work that really matters.

Diego aside, my firm loved me, my work, and my humility! My old boss, Matt, told me he might have a new role for me as they were expanding the gift company to the USA. They would need feet on the street, and I could help with operational set-ups, the same way I had done for them in China. The USA was never really my favourite country, but I was extremely grateful and said yes! Matt, Clara, Diego and I sat down to talk about the details of my transition. I'd work in Brazil for a couple of months before moving to the USA. I'd get a new salary, benefits, job role and KPIs.

We also discussed my handover; Diego would find someone to replace me. Eventually, he decided to hire two people to replace me (imagine how much work I was doing - that itself was validation for me, whether Diego could see it or not). One person would look into all the supply chain stuff, the logistics, the negotiations, and follow-ups, and the other would deal with the company's finances and bureaucracies.

I knew better than to get involved in the recruiting. When you don't make people feel heard, they don't feel like contributing, even though they might be the best people to do so!

I interviewed both of my replacements and gave my opinion, but it didn't really matter what I said. I thought the operations girl he selected was perfect for the role, but the finance guy was not the right fit. He could not do simple maths, did not know what a P&L was, and did not understand cash flow. Why was Diego wanting to hire someone who didn't have a knack for numbers for a role in finance?

I started disliking Diego even more. To me, it doesn't matter whether you're the director, or whatever your title is, if you can't value and respect those who work with you. If you're senior, obviously you have the final say, and you won't always agree with the opinions of your department specialists or your juniors, but that doesn't mean you shouldn't even *listen* to their opinions.

There are the likes of Steve Jobs, who said, *"It doesn't make sense to hire smart people and tell them what to do. We hire smart people so they can tell us what to do."*

And then, there are the likes of Diego!

Anyways, you move on. Pick your battles, right?

I brought my mind back to the present. My China stint really had been one of the best periods of my life, but as I was going to find out, its ending was not going to be smooth by any account.

As soon as I started thinking about my shift to Brazil (looking for a place to stay, and so on), I realised we hadn't closed on my salary for my Brazil stint, so I wrote to Diego for clarification.

I went for a short trip, got back, and still hadn't heard from him, so I wrote to him again, and he again did not answer.

A few months later, tired of sending emails, messages, SMSs and being ignored, I wrote an extensive email expressing my dissatisfaction and my doubts about the next role. Now, this got a response. I was informed my salary while in Brazil would be extremely reduced, and accommodation would not be paid for. This was followed by another shocker: the salary for my USA role was completely changed as well. I found the act extremely disrespectful; I'd never play with someone's life and career in this manner. It's no small thing, moving continents.

In the corporate world (and in life in general), the sad reality is that people will try to walk all over you, and you'll have to say, "no". The higher the stakes, the harder it will feel to stand your ground and maintain the standards of how you are treated. A part of you might even want to give in. But you still have to find it in yourself to say "no", because you will know within yourself that it is the right thing to do.

With my head high, I began negotiations again.

Matt scheduled another discussion call, and I informed Diego of my absolute minimum salary.

The most awful power play followed. It became awfully and disgustingly obvious that he just wanted to show his power over me. He (Diego) said that he had "revisited" my case, and he would accept the pay I wanted, minus approx. $100. He was arguing with me over a difference of just $100! It was not about the money; it was about power, his power to make the final decision, his power to show who was boss and who was subordinate. I was outraged, and I said no.

I repeated my minimum acceptable figure again, slowly losing all excitement in my mind for the role (why would I work for someone like him?) In the end, since they had completely gone back on their word and weren't agreeing to pay me what was acceptable to me, I proposed my final alternative: I needed more time to continue working in China to save the money I would need to make my shift financially possible and viable.

Their options now were to either keep me on in China a little longer or to fire me.

Honestly, I was open to both options, because I'd make money either way. In Brazil, when a company fires someone, they pay them a severance penalty. The person who is fired also gets access to the funds they have contributed to the government-mandated retirement fund. In other words, even if I was fired, I would receive enough money to sustain myself for the next few months.

They decided to fire me.

◆ ◆ ◆

DIARY ENTRY 26

A Journey Within

My time in the Far East was up, and quite suddenly.

I was still processing what had happened, and that I had been fired. At the same time, I could never have imagined how difficult it would be to leave China. I cried a river of tears. Leaving these friends – the memories and feelings – was not easy. The friends I had made in China, from literally all parts of the world, would surprise me with little gestures, written letters, photographs, and even jewellery, and I felt more loved than I had ever felt in my life.

All in all, I decided to put the Diego chapter behind me and leave China with memories of having significantly contributed to the expansion of a foreign organisation, taking back with me a long list of memories, challenges, smiles, tears, and lessons. Onward and upward.

Where in the world would I go next?

I found myself thinking I wouldn't go to the USA, but with a German passport, why not go back to Australia? Europeans have a sweet deal with Australia: they're granted a working visa. The only glitch was that this programme is for those who were under 30 years of age, and I was already 30. I decided to go for it anyway, and it worked out just fine, except that I would get 1 year instead of 2. No payments, no visa application fees, nothing – just an X-ray was needed.

HELL YES!!!! AUSTRALIAAAAA ... I was going back!

Trust yourself, and trust life: remember?

I was trying to figure out where exactly in Australia I'd go, when I heard about "Vipassana," a 10-day silent meditation retreat, somewhere in Bangkok.

I had never been one to shy away from adventure, no matter what shape or form it took, so I signed up for it. Perhaps it would bring me the answers I needed. On the bus to the centre itself, I met two people from Australia also on their way to the experience, and in a few minutes, they had already convinced me to go to Melbourne instead of the Gold Coast, which was my first option.

You may have heard about the Vipassana experience from others, and it seems like everyone emerges from it with stories of a deeply enriching internal journey.

For my part, I took away a rather contradictory bag of thoughts and feelings.

"Make yourself comfortable", was the first sentence the teacher spoke, with the rest of us seated in the meditation room on a few pieces of fabric spread out. Meditating for an entire hour,

uninterrupted, is not easy. Your back hurts. Your leg hurts. Your arm hurts. I think even your nails hurt. But this is supposed to be a part of it. You are supposed to learn that everything is transient, and at some point, will end. The best thing was the "labelling technique": you concentrate on your pain, and tell yourself what it is that is hurting, and how is it hurting. You *observe* the pain, and suddenly, it goes away. I loved it!

Since it's all silent and no one talks to each other, it can be quite a weird vibe. Every day we meditated for 9 hours, which included a walking meditation technique: you concentrate on the energy that is flowing from one leg to another, and meditate with your eyes open. This bit felt like I was in a cheap horror movie where everybody was a zombie. I didn't love it.

As the programme proceeded, I got used to the discomfort of the meditation, and I began loving the silence. No talking to anyone, no greetings, no eye contact ... it really was just me, myself, and I. To my utter surprise, in my zillion hours of meditating in silence, I *didn't* think about things that had happened in the past or worries of the future. I'd just fantasise, like we do when we dream. It was so exciting to watch the thoughts that came up. This bit, again, I loved.

The next day, I felt the need to write my thoughts, to express myself (to talk, somehow, if only to myself!), and the professor would have said it was because I want to "run away" from my mind, and to worry over the "fantasy" that is our life.

Almost every day, I thought of music. One day, the music in my head was from the Brazilian singer Roberto Carlos, who sang that it didn't matter whether he cried or laughed, what mattered is that he *felt* something. And here was our teacher, telling us to keep our mind away from fantasies; when we think about the past, we are trying to fix things, when we think about the future, we are just worrying, and the Buddha teaches us to live in the now, in the present moment.

Finally, the Vipassana ended. I agree that meditation brings calm. But this silent, tranquil life was not for me. I *wanted* to have illusions. I *wanted* to have worries. I *wanted* to cry, to laugh, to sing, to shout, to listen, to interact.

I returned to the real world relieved, my eyes open, my mind eager, and my heart throbbing for my next chapter.

◆ ◆ ◆

DIARY ENTRY 27

Carpe Diem

All right, it was time to move to Australia (again)!

This time, I had a tonne of experience with international work and supply chain operations. Australia is a heavy importer from China, so surely I would get a job in the field in no time (I thought).

Being recently fired and having blown almost all of my earnings and savings on travel, I had just over $7,000 with me, which was just about enough for me to get a plane ticket from Brazil to Australia, pay for a month's rent, and have some pocket-change left over for basic living expenses.

I knew that once I moved back to Australia, I'd most certainly get a job, but it could be at a lower position again, and would probably be based entirely in Australia without much opportunity to travel for work. Plus, Australia was so far away from everywhere else! So if I wanted to travel (which I always did, always do, and always will), now was the time.

My current China company was going to pay for my travel back to Brazil. So why not choose a ticket with a stopover in a country I was yet to see? After a quick check, I found a flight going via South Africa, and I thought "YES! Let's go there!"

You do have to work very, very hard for most things in life. But with others, sometimes, it is just about keeping your eyes and heart open to opportunity.

Whatever it is that you truly seek, you are likely to somehow find, even if it doesn't happen in the exact way you expect it to.

And with that, I found myself in dynamic, multifaceted, and enchanting South Africa!

My days were full of nature, hiking, adventures and even romance. I'd wake up early, have coffee overlooking the ocean, and go walk inside the city. Mossel Bay, where I first stayed, was like a ghost town; all 3 churches I passed by on a Sunday were full, and I would have gone for service too, if I'd been properly dressed. There were two cute restaurants, two small, colourful houses with the brightest green grass a short distance from an ocean that was creating massive waves which a few courageous surfers were taking on. It was the perfect way to pause and unwind, to have days that weren't insanely rushed. I passed not only through Mossel Bay, but also Cape Town, The Crags, Jeffry Bay and Johannesburg. I did my third bungee jump, this time from the world's tallest bridge. If you're wondering, it's very different from how it is in other places – say Macau. It's less professional, you get fewer explanations. It's almost like they put the equipment on you, and 3, 2, 1 ... off you go!

For those of you who've never bungee jumped – I'd describe it as the most heart-pumping activity there is.

My mind went back to my Vipassana experience. Part of it had been all about living in the present moment, fully awake, and whole-heartedly alive. I agree with the essence of this philosophy; unless you bring back your thoughts and emotions to the *now*, you cannot live in the moment fully. Without presence, you cannot seize the day.

But what I've realised is that there are many ways to grab life by the throat and live in the now – and it doesn't have to be something like meditation. Some people I know feel fully alive when they're playing with children and listening to them laugh. Others, when they're deep-sea diving, feeling every single breath, *consciously*.

For me, I felt alive fully with activities such as bungee jumping. In the first few seconds of a bungee jump, even if you try to scream, it's like the voice doesn't leave your mouth. It's just a split second that the adrenaline kicks in, and after that it's pure bliss. When you're going off a bridge, they let you do the "yo-yo" effect until it stops, and you keep hanging there until somebody pulls you up back to the bridge. It's just a jump, but you will feel a blend of fear, excitement, awareness, mindfulness, and even freedom in those few minutes.

When was the last time you did something that made every cell in your body burst with gratitude for being alive? When was the last time you wanted to make every single second count, or you wanted time to stop?

I LOVED every moment of the jump, and before I knew it (as always!) my adventure was over.

We work, we get fired, we find new jobs, we move continents, we find new places to explore, we meet new people, we make new friends, we ruffle some feathers, we meet new loves, we end old loves ... but what matters is that through it all, we *LIVE*.

The author, Joyce Hilfer, explains it beautifully: *"Life is made up of a few moments all strung together like pearls. Each moment is a pearl, and it is up to us to pick the ones with the highest lustre."*

I got home to Brazil just in time for the holidays.

I consciously decided to stay longer; I didn't know how often I could afford to come back to Brazil from Australia. So I spent a heartwarming Christmas and New Year's with my parents.

◆ ◆ ◆

DIARY ENTRY 28

You Only Need to Get It Right Once

The billionaire Mark Cuban has given us a very simple but easy philosophy that deeply resonates with me: *"You only need to get it right once."* In other words, it doesn't matter how many times you fail. With some of the biggest things in life (building a successful business from scratch, getting a dream job, finding your spouse), you can fail 99 times and get it right the 100th time. You can only fail completely, and permanently, *if you give up*.

I would very much need to remember this lesson in the first few days of my return to Australia.

A month before I was due to fly back to the kangaroo land, from Brazil, I started looking for jobs.

My focus was clear: I'd stick to the supply chain and logistics space. Perhaps the best aspect of my work in China (and the reason I didn't burn out) was that I had had my weekends free, with the exception of the Canton fairs. This had allowed me the time, energy, and desire to build and maintain other aspects of life outside of work: friendships, relationships, and time with myself.

With this in mind, I applied for several jobs – I don't remember the exact number, but it must have been around 40. For most, I would just receive an automatic message saying, *"Thanks for your application, we will be in touch"*. For a small percentage of these, actual humans would get back days later, but still with a, *"We regret to inform you that for this position we've selected someone else"*.

I know, firsthand, how disheartening this process can be. You've got to keep remembering your past successes, replaying them in your head.

Finally, two recruiters did engage with me in longer conversations about my skills. Again here, there was the problem that they needed someone right away and they were not willing to wait for me to get to Australia.

I chose to consider this headway in my job hunt as a win, believing I really would get a job soon, and decided to resume this process once I was back on Australian ground. After all, I only needed to get it right once!

I had incredible work experience from China, and was perhaps the best person ever to work with Chinese suppliers. With a German passport (which meant a work visa) and Australia's dependency on Chinese imports, I knew I'd be coveted by Australian organisations.

I was mindful that my English still wasn't the best. I had a lot of experience conversing in English with the Chinese and with my friends, but none with native English speakers. Even so, I trusted in my own worth as an employee, and after all, whatever English I needed to get by in Australia would probably be for conversation with the Chinese anyway.

If someone just gave me an interview, I would get the job.

◆ ◆ ◆

DIARY ENTRY 29

There Is a Time to Fight, and a Time to Flow

Ah, Australia, that magical land! How happy I was to be there again!

I rented a bedroom in an Airbnb for a month, in a neighbourhood an hour away from Melbourne by train, with some dollars in my savings account.

It was a perfect, sunny Sunday, not hot, not cold – so I walked around, watching people sitting on the park grass, eating their lunch, playing with their kids, laughing, listening to music, and dancing.

The first Monday back, I resumed with the job applications.

One has to be aggressive, and I was applying for 10-15 positions every day, reaching some with a generic cover letter, others with a tailored one ... and got an interview with a company that imported furniture from China.

The interview went extremely well, and I was thrilled. I stood out, as expected, because of my Chinese work experience of many years.

And then I received a piece of news that shook me to my core.

We were wrapping up, discussing the visa situation, and I proudly stated that there was nothing to worry about: I had a working holiday visa for one entire year. And my recruiter replied that he could *not* hire me with a working holiday visa – that sort of visa allowed a foreigner to work for the same company for just 6 months and, unfortunately, he could not invest that much time and energy in me knowing I'd have to leave in 6 months.

I'd had no idea! I decided not to believe him, and went about my own research, which only confirmed what he had said. It slowly sunk in: why would any company hire me for just 6 months? If it made no sense to me, how could I convince an interviewer?

I would have to think of something else – and soon enough, I did.

I hadn't always been in the supply chain space; I had once been the most badass events manager in town! Events is what I would go back to. I could engage in projects, their planning, in the post-event tasks – there's a lot I could do to contribute.

And so the hunt began (again).

You only needed to get it right once – remember?

After reading a tonne of *"You have not been selected"* messages and submitting more and more applications, I stumbled upon an opportunity for *"Events Director"*.

The word "Director" would have scared me off, but this job description had something different: they wanted the application to be sent by a recorded video.

I jumped out of bed and put on a formal jacket on top of my PJs. I positioned my phone on my bed and recorded my video. With what I know was infectious enthusiasm, I explained where I was from, my experience with events in Brazil, my past few years in China, and how grateful I would be if I got a chance to get interviewed.

The next day I received an email to schedule a phone interview. A phone interview! That was different, but exciting.

The call went just fine, and I spoke directly to the CEO. I did not understand his English fully, but he would repeat his questions, and I would answer as confidently as I could in my broken English. In another two days, I received an invitation for an in-person interview with Pablo, the CEO (who I'd report to), and Josh, the current General Manager (who I'd be taking over from).

To prepare for the interview, I needed to describe how I'd managed previous events from idea creation through to ticket sales, demonstrate my time management process, create a 3-day sample retreat for 10 VIP clients with costs, explain what I'd do with a hypothetical one million dollars to be used in a week, talk about my mentors, and myself. This was easy-peasy for me, and I truly enjoyed my days before the interview, preparing my presentation and pulling out real quotes from suppliers.

The presentation began – and I remember Josh was super engaged, but Pablo would be looking at his phone, and then sometimes at me, and sometimes to nowhere. (Later, I discovered this technique was used to gauge my emotional intelligence and observe my reaction under pressure.) When I finished, Pablo would lighten up, ask me a few questions, and leave me with Josh to answer my questions. Josh clarified that the work would be arduous, and I presented my case of hard work in Brazil and long hours in China, and pacified him, assuring him I was not scared to work, at all.

(Sure, I wasn't happy to be working weekends, but I'd figure that bit out. For now, I just really wanted the job – I had bills piling up, and I truly believed I could do this work well.)

That night I received a call asking me to return the next morning for the final interview and decision. That last day, I was pitted in a room together with Alessio, my competitor for the role; I could immediately see that Alessio was the smooth talker, the sales type of guy, and I was the operations girl.

I didn't want anyone to feel misled, so I clarified my visa situation from the outset. Luckily for me, Pablo ran several companies and could simply jump me from one to another, so on paper, I'd be working for different entities – visa problem solved.

I got the job! Actually, we *both* got the job. They made a new sales position for Alessio, and the events operations one was given to me.

That feeling of getting a job you really want – there are no words to capture it. I was going to be an "Events Director" in Australia! I remembered how I had left China and everything I had felt at the time ... the anger, the nervousness, the fear, and among it all, the little bit of hope.

I accepted and signed the job offer the very next day. I received a bottle of champagne, some flowers, and a company iPhone, and discovered that my annual salary would be $50,000 dollars.

In a stark variation from my experiences with the Chinese, up until that point, my potential Australian employer had not brought up the subject of money, so I really was surprised and extremely happy. In China, I'd been making something like $36,000 dollars, at the most.

I think it's always important to remember that *change* is the only real constant in life.

We can try and try, but we cannot foresee everything, bad or good.

We can be extremely strong and determined, but we cannot win by fighting every time.

We navigate through life, sometimes hating change, other times loving it, sometimes resisting it, other times embracing it ... But when we don't have answers and choose to go with the flow, it can bring us to extraordinary destinations.

If you're never brave enough to surrender to the currents of transformation, how can you hope to stumble into possibilities that are outside of your mind?

You cannot go to where your wildest dreams are, and where wonderful opportunities lie in wait, unless you do both: *Fight* for what you truly want (when you need to), and *Flow* towards your desires in the way life makes you (when you have to).

◆ ◆ ◆

DIARY ENTRY 30

Practise What You Preach

In March 2016, I step into my first day at the Pablo Grey Coaching, with Pablo as my boss.

There is no way I could have known then how much I would learn from Pablo, and how much interacting with him, and even just observing him, would come to shape my mindset.

Pablo made his money by coaching others. At the time, he was mainly coaching real estate players. The coaching would be either with recurring clients paying $8,000 per hour for a coaching call per month (the insanely high value impressed me), or in one-off calls.

My new team and office were both super small. There was just one table with Pablo, Alessio, another Brazilian guy who was also newly hired to be a social media person, and myself.

As my first task, Pablo gave me a "bootcamp" event to organise - it would be his first, and I needed to get started with venues. I was extremely embarrassed to call the hotels in front of him due to my lack of confidence in speaking English. A few times I would even pretend to continue a conversation over a phone call that had already ended (dropped on the other side, because I did not understand a word that was being spoken). When he wasn't around, however, and I was alone or in the corridor, I would put my embarrassment aside and just do my job. I'd speak in broken English, ask as many questions as I needed to ask, and make them repeat their answers.

I grew to respect Pablo, mainly because not many people practise what they preach to others. Pablo not only did, but he also made his livelihood that way!

Sometimes I would pay attention to the coaching calls themselves – what advice was Pablo giving to his clients?

One thing I learnt was that Pablo would tell his clients they needed to hire someone to answer their phones, to say they were "not available". He would finish the call saying he himself didn't know if he still had time to continue his call with them, and that they'd need to check with his assistant for a slot in his calendar first.

He was teaching his clients a technique to get more business by creating scarcity of supply where there was a demand, and then immediately applying the exact same technique on them!

It was bold, but it worked. I disliked seeing everyone going after their clients in this way – but hey, nothing is perfect.

◆ ◆ ◆

DIARY ENTRY 31

See, Learn, Repeat

Just a week after I started, Pablo signed a contract to go speak in Cyprus. I hadn't been in Australia even 2 months, and off I was, flying away already.

I would not organise the event per se, just the logistics for me and Pablo. We would be staying at the same hotel that was holding the conference. I had to buy the air tickets, check the visa stuff, arrange for transportation, and always make sure there were enough bottles of Fiji Water and bananas – which Pablo could simply not do without.

We got to Cyprus, and I had already made my first mistake.

It was clear that I had not done my research fully. You see, Cyprus is an island country, in the middle of the Mediterranean Sea. For the rest of the world, it is one country. It is, however, divided into two parts: a Turkish side, and a Greek side, and they hate each other. It seems the Turkish side had declared its independence, but that had not been accepted internationally. If you were born on the island, you could cross both sides, but if you were from Turkey, you couldn't go to the Greek side, and vice-versa. Me, blissfully unaware of this, had decided to fly us to the airport which was closer to the event venue, but *it was on the wrong side of the split*. Which meant Pablo needed a visa to cross over from one side to the other (I was okay because of my German passport).

Luckily, it didn't get as bad as it might have. All we needed was to show the reason why we wanted to go to the Turkey side, and I had the speaking engagement contract with me. We also showed our return tickets out of Cyprus, and these were enough. We got Pablo the necessary visa on the spot. After the visa situation sorted, we left with the driver. It was bizarre: our driver would literally stop the car, remove the number plate of the Greek side, fix on another one from the Turkish side, and continue the trip!

Lesson learnt: always do your homework.

Pablo's birthday was the next day after the keynote speech, and I needed to organise some things in a couple of hours while he was preparing to be on stage. So off we went, me and the security guard, to find a birthday breakfast spot. I learnt quickly there that Turkish men like to talk shop with other men and don't respond well to women. If I would ask if we could have breakfast ready at 9:00 am instead of 10:00 am, and we would pay extra, they'd say no to me, but they eventually said yes to the guard. It seems Turkish men don't want to take any kind of requests or orders from women, even if she is a client.

Another lesson learnt: Understand and play along with local culture, it'll help you get things done faster.

Meanwhile, Pablo's wife contacted me, asking if I would please print a picture of his daughter and give it to him, together with a piece of cake, in the morning. When I asked the hotel where I could print the picture, someone gave me the idea of making an entire cake with the picture of his daughter imprinted on it. I did that, and I am so glad! Early on his birthday morning he was surprised by the hotel staff knocking on his door with balloons and a cake with his daughter's face printed on it. Not only were Pablo and his wife thrilled and extremely happy, but I also sensed a shift in Pablo's trust in me.

Before we knew it, the Cyprus event was over.

After Cyprus, my next events would be around Australia, in Melbourne, Sydney and Brisbane. One of Pablo's partners, Max, was a real estate coach who would sell his courses and mentoring to the audience, but there was no one better in sales than the sales king, Pablo Grey. So they'd craft an offer together, with Pablo on stage for 3 hours, ending the talk with a sale that involved mentorship from Max and a coaching call with Pablo.

I truly learnt a lot about sales from just being with and being around Pablo.

Take, for instance, the paperwork. It included a form already half filled out with the pricing struck through and new pricing written down below, because the audience were being sold a "promotional price." Newly converted clients' names, addresses and credit card information would be meticulously recorded, with bottles of champagne as gifts from Pablo for those who had decided to act.

Things were thought out to the last detail. The air conditioning: It was a must for people to be freezing. If the temperature was comfortable, people fell asleep. If it was cold, they would remain alert.

And Pablo was indeed *really* good on stage. He would capture the attention of everybody and deliver a mix of mindset boosts and sales techniques. At the end, he would do his little sales pitch and, just like clockwork, convert a minimum of 30% of the people present in the room every time. The package cost sold to them was $AU3,996.

He even made it a little dramatic: he would say that had just 10 slots available, so you needed to move fast, and the audience would run to the back of the room, where I would be waiting with forms and pens ready to roll the sales. He would include a timer on the 2 massive screens. "Just 5 minutes, don't miss the opportunity!"

It was obviously an artificial urgency he created, but we would sell as many as we could.

I was learning a great deal from Pablo, but at the same time Alessio was making things harder for me.

He was slow, he would lie about his performance, saying he had called x number of people when had only called y, while taking up the front and centre spot with Pablo, talking sweetly to his face and harshly behind his back.

I already knew by then that reality shows itself over time.

Alessio however, just like a little kid, would go behind my back to Pablo to talk bad things about me: my English was not good enough, I didn't know what I was doing, and so on. The pressure was real. Pablo caught me crying in the corridor one day, and I told him I was doing my best, and he just said to not worry. He liked me, and I should just keep going.

With Alessio, it would get worse, and then it would just end.

We went to Singapore for another event, and Alessio was acting like a celebrity himself. He would go eat in fancy restaurants, rent a fancy car, and since I oversaw the budget and logistics, I did not approve his unjustified expenses. On top of everything, when we returned, I saw that he was inflating expenses in his favour to receive more money. I could not stand it and flagged that to Pablo in front of Alessio. Hot-headed, the three of us went into a meeting room to discuss this terrible relationship. Alessio looked at Pablo and said if I was to continue in the team, he would be out. From that moment on, Alessio was out.

We talked about it before and I want to reinforce a lesson: keep your head down, and do the work, no matter what others say. Work speaks for itself when the time comes. Keep your character in check, no matter what others do. Character always shows for itself when the time comes.

◆ ◆ ◆

DIARY ENTRY 32

My Fool-Proof Formula

After coming back to Australia, even before getting a job, I had started researching getting permanent residency in the country. I kind of had to – I just had a 1-year permit to work, and I wanted to live in Australia permanently.

Amongst all the pathways I could choose to get my residency (including investing in the country and getting married), the one that suited me best was to have a company that would sponsor this process. With this route, you needed a high level of education and work experience in your chosen field – and I had both. I was a postgraduate with an MBA, and I had 8 years of experience in events and 3 years of experience in the supply chain space. I had a strong case!

Do you remember the formula I recommended earlier to grow at work? Know your worth and find a way to ask for it. You can ask for more money, but if you think this won't be palatable to your employer, or if something else is more important to you at the time, ask for that. But go ahead and just *ask*.

I already knew as soon as I got to Australia that I'd ask whoever I started working for to sponsor me. That's also why I've always cared very little about starting salaries in new roles - I have confidence in myself, and I grow in salary positions every single time. I know what I have to do: show my work and ask for more.

Exactly three months after started working for Pablo, I approached him with the residency idea.

It was an investment of $AU15,000. We would begin the process, and the visa application basically entailed waiting for answers. It gave me all the working rights, and we would not need to change employers. Pablo would not have to do much besides sign some paperwork and obviously pay for the process.

Pablo said yes, and my residency process started.

◆ ◆ ◆

DIARY ENTRY 33

More Money, More Lessons

2016: What a year!

For the second half of the year, all events were in Asia. The Singapore event had brought Pablo into the limelight and left him strongly imprinted in the minds of those at a firm called Your Success. Your Success worked with a tonne of speakers, but nobody would sell more than Pablo, and since the company gained 40% of each speaker's sales, it was great for them to have Pablo around.

Sales events were what we called "Front-end Events," and longer events where the public could experience more of the speaker, were called "Back-end Events" – like bootcamps. We would do front-end events in Singapore, Malaysia, Thailand, and Vietnam, selling them the follow-up back-end events.

Those tours looked amazing on the outside – flying to beautiful Asian countries, all expenses paid for – but in reality, they were a LOT of hard work. I sure learnt more and more from Pablo, but the tours were back-breaking, non-stop work that often left me physically sick with a weekend in bed, unable to move.

We were a team doing the tours. Alessio and the other social media guy had left, but it was still me, Pablo, and Sammy, who was a new hire. Sammy was your typical Australian: gorgeous, with long blonde hair and blue eyes, and a very hard worker.

From the moment we'd land, it was "go-time". In the country visits, we'd often catch up with Michael and Alex. Michael was an old client that Pablo had helped to become wealthy. He would genuinely just come to help, acting as a security guard, and finding out all the back ways from the hotel room to the stage.

(No matter where he went, Pablo would have a security guard. It was a psychological technique to trick people into believing he was a celebrity and a very important person.)

The first stop on the tour was Singapore. Pablo was flying business class, while I was in economy, carrying everything: the flip chart, the banners, the sales forms, the microphone, the pens. I hadn't forgotten the Fiji Water and bananas for Pablo.

Technically, we should have had to pay for extra luggage, but Pablo had a trick to teach me here.

I would put all our stuff in the weighing machine, and Pablo would strike up a conversation with the attendant, complimenting her on her hair, or her clothes, or her nails ... anything, really, that would shift her attention from the logical left side of her brain to the emotional right side. Why? Because while he was chatting, he was also lifting the weight machine with his pointy shoes, which meant the weight machine would then blink at a much lower weight, in which case the lady attendant would check the numbers. If she was receiving a compliment, she was happy, and she wasn't paying much attention to the numbers. Not a single time did we pay for the extra weight.

Again, I know this was not ideal, and not something I'd have thought of myself. But it certainly was helpful.

We'd land the same day as the event, I would check Pablo in, go to the event venue, and count the number of chairs. This number was very important for Pablo. His agreement with Your Success was based on performance, so chairs and headcount mattered. Pablo often asked me to also include the headcount numbers of the other speakers. He was one step ahead on several other things as well – testing the microphone and speakers in advance, for instance.

Mental note (next lesson from Pablo): leave nothing to chance, especially when you can be prepared.

Pablo would come down to the green room just minutes before his talk, deliver it, sell the minimum expected of 30% of the room, and we would go straight to the airport to fly to the next country.

I'd have absolutely no "free time". While at the airport, I needed to log the sales into the system and process the payments. All those people we had sold to would later need to receive a welcome phone call, a confirmation of their online course, as well as a mention of event participation and the name of the person they would bring as their plus one, which we did in order to have a full house. On top of all this work, I was in charge of the team's flight schedules, accommodation, commute cars ...

I would go to bed at about 1:00 am or 2:00 am, and be up at 7:00 am. And off we'd go again to the next country. Fiji Water, bananas, champagne, sales forms, sound check ... Next stop: Malaysia. Next: Thailand. Final stop: Vietnam.

And at long last, we were back in Australia.

◆ ◆ ◆

DIARY ENTRY 34

Get Used to Exceeding Expectations

I learnt early on that at work, delivering the bare minimum won't always be enough. It can get you by, in the sense that you may not get fired, but if you only do specifically what you're told to do without really applying yourself, you won't go places.

If you want to grow, and truly shine at your job no matter what you do, I'd suggest getting into the habit of exceeding expectations.

This means you've got to do what you are explicitly *told* needs to be done, *and* what is *implied* needs to be done. I promise you, most people on the planet struggle even with the former, and a very small percentage master the latter.

If you decide to do both, you will be unstoppable. And the best way for you to be able to do both is by feeling a sense of ownership - by embracing the responsibility of your role.

Take the case of my bootcamps with Pablo. These would happen after the "sales" or "front-end" tours were over; from our 3 tours around Asia, we confirmed some 150 to 200 people, depending on the country, to attend each of the 3 bootcamps.

In total, each bootcamp required a tonne of work I was told to do - each event would involve a total of 5 days of work in each country, with 16 to 20 hours of work per day.

This is what that more or less looked like:

Day Zero:
The day prior to the event was for setting up.

The usual set up was school style with tables and chairs. Name badges would be allocated inside the room, workbooks would be ready to be provided, and the arrangement of people would be as planned - paid people up front, guests at the back. All bootcamp events would need some translation system as well, because locals didn't always know English well. I needed to provide translation services and headsets for every single person. There was the sound check, learning the back ways in the venue, and of course, the hustle for the Fuji waters and bananas. The set up would be done by around 11:00 pm.

Remember, when you pay attention to your work and you're extremely good at it, people sort of start to expect that - so by this point, a lot of the work I was doing behind the scenes was pretty much "autopilot" stuff for Pablo.

Day One:
The event itself would start the next day at 7:00 am, which meant I was awake from 6:00 am and would be up till 2:00 am on stage days:

no kidding. Me and Pablo would be communicating via WhatsApp the entire time. He would always be pushing for the air conditioning to be colder (it was never cold enough for him), and for me to be faster running the microphone while he interacted with people.

All explicit instructions handled? Check!

Pablo wanted me inside the room at all times. Yep: no breaks!

I would have to be there opening and closing doors for people coming in and out, while somehow handling the zillion other things that had nothing to do with the stage. For example, we'd also be communicating about lunchtime. He would ask for it to be prepared for 1:00 pm, then for 4:00 pm, which would make the hotel people extremely mad at me, and me mad at Pablo: why change the time so many times? Why make it so late? (Pablo had his reasons, he'd do this to prove to people the power of their minds). By the third time this happened with Pablo I had learnt his pattern, and I started telling the hotels we would not go for lunch before 3:00 pm. Even if Pablo told me we would, I would pretend I had scheduled it for the time he asked for, but I would already have scheduled it for later. I thought the stress caused by me having to change times with the hotel all the time was unnecessary.

Implied needs met, in addition to expected deliverables? Check!

Day Two:
We'd be on a roll by now.

The next morning, Pablo would grab a massage and prepare himself to speak on stage the entire afternoon, all the way to midnight. The event itself would start at 8:00 am and I would be up from 7:00 am. If you remember, I had gone to bed at around 3:00 am so it means resting for just 4 hours. But I had to face the exhaustion and keep smiling.

Pablo would be checking with me how the vibe was in the room the entire morning and always wanted me to make sure the audience was all pumped up before he arrives back on the stage.

Day 2 would finish at around midnight and I finally would get a 6 hour sleep until next day.

Persevering through exhaustion and still delivering? Check!

Day Three:
Sales day!

It was time to make money again - and obviously, Pablo was addicted to sales. While the other speaker would be on stage, Pablo would be conducting "interviews" with people interested in his inner circle mentorship programme, which cost around $40K/ year. By 8:00 pm or later, he would come on stage to deliver the conclusion of the bootcamp.

Navigating the high-pressure sales day? Check!

The Last Day:
Wrap-up time. I would have to pack it all up, and we would fly back to Australia.

In case you were wondering, event logistics can be very similar across different geographies, and even though each country has its own unique challenges, all of them roll pretty much the same way. But in general, believe me when I say that planning boot camps can entail a whole new level of exhaustion.

The only way I was able to excel at my job, was (as I mentioned previously) because of my sense of responsibility towards my work.

If I didn't feel the level of ownership I did, I wouldn't care as much, I wouldn't work as hard, and things would now and then just go completely off track.

I know that "being responsible" or "feeling ownership" sound like simple concepts. And yet, in the vast expanse of the professional world, they remain some of the rarest and most valuable qualities.

Staying on top of your role, being true to your word, and exceeding expectations can make all the difference. And this involves the simple stuff which most people take for granted: communicating well at all times, honouring your commitments, and keeping everyone in the loop when unforeseen circumstances arise.

Responsibility and ownership combined will earn you the trust and respect of those around you - which is something *many* will fail at getting.

You will grow, while others will stay where they are.

◆ ◆ ◆

DIARY ENTRY 35

More Confidence = More Comfort

A typical month during my work with Pablo usually involved 2 weeks in Melbourne, and 2 weeks travelling.

When we weren't travelling, normal work hours were 8:00 am to 6:00 pm, but I would stay in until at least 8:00 pm. So naturally, I did not have a lot of time for fun or for friends. The friend I did have was Alexander, a gay guy who had come to share the house I had moved into.

Previously, it had been me, the house owner (an Australian), and another lady from New Zealand. The Australian woman at first was a great friend, but as time went by her habits got to me. She would go out often, get drunk, bring men home and knock at my door at 2:00 am, asking for my help to remove them from the house ... I was of course okay with helping her, but with my insane work, I would be tired. I could do without that noise and craziness. The New Zealand lady, on the other hand, was great, but she couldn't stand the Australian either and she left, which is when Alexander moved in. He had a boyfriend from Italy, Luca. And for that whole year to come, they would be my only two friends.

After a few more months, I couldn't stand the Australian lady anymore myself! I started looking for my own apartment – but that would mean I needed a bump in my salary. It was time to apply my same formula for growth once again: proving my worth – and asking to be paid for it.

After having handled several tours around Asia and Pacific as well as several bootcamps, I had enough proof of my capabilities. I sat with Pablo once again and asked for more money, which resulted in an increase from $AU50K per year to $AU80K per year. In the corporate world, if you just push yourself a bit harder at work (which not many others will do), you can build more confidence. This, in turn, can help you ask for way more money than you presently make, so that you can live the comfortable life you deserve.

The apartment I got was great! It was a one-bedroom on St Kilda beach; I bought all the furniture myself and decorated it my own way. It feels so good to have your own space, doesn't it? Having my own home also drove a bunch of new romances in the beginning – I liked and dated 2 or 3 guys simultaneously. There was this surfer guy I liked a lot, but he mainly just wanted to sleep with me. And there was this Italian who really liked me and was good to me, buying flowers and cooking for me, but I let him pass; I suppose I was okay with keeping it casual.

As time passed, these romances faded away, and once again, work took the forefront.

◆ ◆ ◆

DIARY ENTRY 36

When Did You Last Count Your Gifts?

Ok, so I had gotten a raise, but through all of 2017, work at Pablo Grey Coaching remained just outright crazy.

There was not a single time that I didn't end up sick in bed after a tour. My life was just about working, working, and working some more, or sleeping at home. Even my meals would be eaten with my eyes glued to the computer if we were in the office, or a quick bite of some junk at an airport while on tour. The team size increased, which meant more logistics to organise for everyone, which meant more responsibility – which obviously, I liked to deliver on.

Sure, with a larger team and more helping hands, you can have some breaks (say, a 20-minute break in a 20-hour long workday). But those breaks were not the relaxation you would expect: if, say, we didn't have the hotel for an extra night, we'd be resting on the floor of a breakout room or the equivalent.

Life was just work, and I was starting to dislike the conditions. It had been a year and a half, and I had started thinking about leaving the group.

I had arrived at a pivot point again – and that got me thinking. Was I rushing, and taking decisions quickly? Or was I actually flowing with life and its motions - living and working through every phase, its unique process, its ups and downs - and developed a sort of pattern to my life?

I realised (to my relief), that it was the latter.

I had grown used to reflecting on my life every now and then, and I wish the same for you. You have only one life, and it goes by quickly. You don't have to stay on the exact same track if you aren't happy, and reflection helps you stay true to your core values and adjust your goals.

Here is the reflection I recorded in my diary:

I had taken my time, back in Brazil, when I was thinking about leaving. And after I made the decision, I had still given myself 6 months to plan. That was when the universe sent me a friend who had connected me with the representative role in China.

China! How extraordinary the Far East had been! When in my life could I have imagined anything like it? I had loved the idea and made it work, spending almost 3 years in Asia, learning a tonne, visiting and setting up factories, riding trains and motorcycles with other Chinese people thousands of times, travelling to some 20 new countries, and making unforgettable friendships.

It was in my second year in China that I started thinking about moving again, not because of some childish or rash decision, but because

I genuinely felt my stint had run its course, and it was time to begin a new chapter in life. That time, the universe had gifted me with a German passport. And even with a job offer in the United States, I had decided to return to Australia (with the option of a working holiday visa with the European passport). The decision came, and again, it took me around 6 months to organise everything.

I had come to Australia without a job and with little money. And again, in three weeks, I had made everything work: housing and a job. Within three months I had began my residency process, and within 6 months, I had rented my own beachside apartment. I had visited 5 new countries on countless trips. I had taken up skateboarding and broken my nose (a story for another time). Sure, things always happened quickly when I arrived at a place, but I did spend my share of time and reflection planning for what came next.

Now I had been a year and a half in Australia, and the call to leave had arisen within me again. The whole wide world was calling, again!

I had millions of business ideas.

I had thousands of options for countries to go to.

I had no specific answers yet (as always!) but my decision had been made: I will leave by April 2018, having completed two years with Pablo, and with my residency in my hands.

When you reflect, (and please do so frequently on your career path), you learn to see the gifts the universe has been bringing you. Knowing that the universe has your back just helps you live life with much more faith, rather than fear. You don't need all the answers. No one ever has all the answers (no matter how much they pretend). But once you really decide and commit to a course, the universe starts to help. It brings you the people you need, and the opportunities you can't even imagine.

You have to truly trust that you can achieve the outcome, and then the universe co-creates with you.

◆ ◆ ◆

DIARY ENTRY 37

Amidst Reality, Choose Gratitude

Choosing a mindset of gratitude can really change your perspective on day-to-day life.

One day, I witnessed a discussion between one of my work colleagues and my boss, Pablo.

She was arguing that she had put in 300 hours of extra work. He was arguing that what she receives in return from the company was enough to compensate for it: she had gained a salary increase, she had a day in lieu for every weekend day she worked, she could leave early on days she went to university ...

It made me think ... Yes, we *were* working really intensely. But we did get small things in return, for which, if we chose to be, we really could be grateful for.

In my case, I got a few tickets for my vacations, and I got my residency process all paid for. I was learning things about business no university would teach me! The effort that goes into succeeding in business, the respect you need for the processes, the art of sales, the strategy marketing, having a knack for numbers and observing the margin of the businesses: how else would I ever learn all this?

I could choose to complain about the hours, or I could choose to be grateful for the perks.

What would you have done? I decided to be grateful.

My mind went back to where I was 5 years ago. I was working almost just as hard, in Brazil. At the time, this role of "Global Events Director" in Australia, making the money I was making, would have been a bizarre, faraway, insane dream!

I wasn't lying to myself about the money. Yes, I needed to change my money mindset. You can't make more money if you think what you get is enough, right? But, hey, for now, it was paying my bills, I had my own place, and I was doing way better than I could have ever dreamt. So yes, of course I was grateful for my job.

I don't know anyone who goes through life without moments of internal conflict and conversation like this. But I do know that it helps a LOT to consciously develop a habit of feeling grateful for what you have *now*, even when you know for sure you can do better *tomorrow*.

◆ ◆ ◆

DIARY ENTRY 38

When in Rome, Take Notes from the Romans

All through 2017, events continued in Australia, but thankfully, events in Asia had stopped.

With all the commission we had to pay for Your Success, there hadn't been much left for us, but it had been decent visibility for Pablo. I was very happy. After all, I had left Asia to come to Australia, and I really wanted to experience more of Oceania. And I was happy with what I was learning working at the office with Pablo.

We've all heard: when in Rome, do as the Romans do. I second this: it helps to take copious notes from the Romans (even if you won't use them all). Who knows if you'll be back in Rome again?

My "Rome" was Pablo Grey Coaching.

I've already given you loads of small examples of small things I picked up working alongside Pablo day in and day out – here are a few more invaluable lessons.

#1 – Build the Sales Cycle

In January 2017 we moved to bigger premises with a separate office for Pablo, a meeting room, a studio room, and the main, open-plan office with desks and chairs for some 10 people. This housed our new accountant, 2 guys for sound and video, a designer, and an events producer to assist me.

Pablo had had this brilliant idea to create front events himself (without depending on another group like Your Success), to sell boot camps around Australia. As was everything he did, this was smart. First, he would hire a big name, say a co-founder of Netflix, and market the event on Facebook. He would charge almost nothing, like $AU20 for the invitee plus one. People would go to the event to hear the keynote speaker, but surprise, surprise! Pablo would be on stage prior to that, and obviously, crush it with his sales. The more people that would attend this event, the more conversions we'd have for boot camp.

Additionally, Pablo decided to leverage the tours that his real estate coaching partner was already running to do his own event: "An Evening with Pablo Grey". For me, this meant in a single week we would have 8 events in 4 different cities in Australia (sometimes adding Auckland in New Zealand too). And this would happen once a month! Just think about how insane this was.

Anyways, the front-end event would sell into bootcamps – we would have 1 boot camp every 3 months. And at the bootcamp, we would sell an "Inner Circle" programme, so now, there was also the Inner Circle events to take care of, which in a year included 4 conferences and a party extravaganza.

We sold *everything* we did – at front-end events, we sold bootcamps, at bootcamps we sold the programme, and with all the buzz, we sold more of the front-end events ...

That, ladies and gentlemen, is how you create a sales cycle.

#2 – Remember What Matters

By January 2018, I had seen loads of people coming and loads of people leaving, while I was the standing rock at the group.

I kept reminding myself of what kept me going. I reminded myself of my residency visa. So many people could only dream of a shot at an Australian Residency Card, and I had it! The job was insane, tiring, even unfair, but at the same time, I knew I could not quit.

#3 – ASK. The Worse That Can Happen Is That You'll Hear a "No"

With all the work I was putting in, one thing Pablo would not take away from my mind is that I deserved more money.

For the third time now, I went to negotiate my salary with him and he agreed.

It was another 55% jump, from $AU80K per year to $AU125K per year.

That was enough for me to start saving some money, I thought. Or perhaps to try to build a business on the side ...

#4 – People *Like* Theatrics

Pablo was a human being that always intrigued me – whether in a good way or bad, I couldn't initially tell.

I'm sure you've come across such people as well.

He was, for real, the ultimate sales guy. He could sell an igloo house to an Eskimo in Alaska, *and* charge them extra for the iced water, if you asked him to.

He could sell anything to anyone – he could manipulate people's minds in a way that was scary. Back in 2016, when it was only him, me, and Sammy, he had booked us into a marvellous Airbnb for a retreat, and it had indeed been a good experience. But the bizarre thing was that he would go live on social media, saying he was having a company retreat with his team of 20+ members, playing basketball and having massages, which was all a lie. I honestly think that perhaps he didn't *mean* to lie; he just brainwashed himself about all of that being real. On cruise parties with clients, Sammy and I knew we were expected to lie and say we were a bigger company.

For parties, Pablo would arrive by helicopter, pretending to come from an important "venture capital meeting", when in fact we had hired the chopper from just a few miles away – and a car would have been faster!

He kept up the theatrics because, as it turned out, people bought them.

#5 – Borderline Unethical (or Not?)

I observed everything Pablo did to grow, but that doesn't mean I approved or agreed with it all.

I found much of his work ethic to be something to be sceptical about.

Yes, he did get better clients, and some clients did get better results – but this was mostly true of real estate and service-related business. Outside of these, even though he now sold to *everyone*, I didn't really see Pablo being able to help.

As I observed Pablo's growth, I couldn't fully endorse his work ethic. Though he achieved success in certain areas, I questioned his ability to help beyond specific niches. Nevertheless, it's essential to remember that everyone bears responsibility for their actions. Passing judgement may not reveal the true value of what he offered. In a world where accountability matters, each individual's choices shape their journey, and only time can truly assess their impact.

#6 - "Fake It Till You Make It"

My personal feelings towards Pablo's success aside, he really was succeeding before my eyes.

The offers were becoming more expensive. He was getting more clients. He was changing offices. He was actually hiring more people. This time, when he did a company retreat, there really were 10+ people.

Pablo used to lie about where he lived, but now, he really did move to a mansion in a great location in Melbourne. He used to lie about being a multimillionaire, and now he really was a multi-millionaire.

#7 - To Sell or to Trick?

I wanted to convince myself that if everything was happening to Pablo was because he deserved it. But the fact is that I never felt comfortable about it all.

The worst for me was the sales technique we used in the boot camp to the inner circle programme.

On the first day, Pablo would strategically mention the programme here and there during the boot camp, making people curious. Meanwhile, the current inner circle members would be treated like kings in front of everyone else.

On the second day, he would say the inner circle was open for applications, and he would play a video. And even someone like me, who knew exactly what all went on behind the scenes, would buy into that video! I found myself pretty much saying: *"Here, take all my money," or "I'll work for you for free, but please coach me, you are amazing!"* I'd be completely mesmerised.

But his sales pitch wouldn't end there. Next, he'd ask the people who were interested to please see him at lunch the following day. We would, in advance, rent a small breakout room (a smaller room makes it feel like more people are inside, and makes you think others want the same thing you want).

In this breakout session, he would mention the price and say that only a small group of people would be "selected". He'd ask for forms to be filled out.

I hated that in this entire 20-page application form, in which we asked everything you can possibly imagine about people's businesses, their dreams, and their ideas, we would only care about one page: the page where they would select how they would pay for the programme if chosen, whether in full, or in 12 instalments. All the forms would come to me, and it was my job to signal to Pablo who would pay in full, and who would take the payment plans. Pablo would only want to talk with the ones who chose payment in full.

Day 3 of the boot camp would technically be entirely for this "interview" process.

As for the interviews, I was not in the room when Pablo conducted them, but I know what went on: Pablo would ask the client why they wanted to be part of the programme *instead of the client interviewing Pablo as to what he could do for them.*

You see the trick here? It's getting the person who wants to buy the programme to convince you, the seller, to accept him or her. We would sell the "Inner Circle Program" to another 12 to 15 people.

In everybody's eyes, Pablo was this big-hearted, genuine guy wanting to help. In my eyes, he was a thorough businessman who mainly worried about his sales and his money.

#8 - Make People Feel Great about Themselves

Whether Pablo was indeed interested in making others succeed or not is a mystery. I like to think that perhaps at least in some way, he was.

But even that involved brainwashing. He would, for example, invite clients who had experienced a small success onto stage, and make them feel like kings of the world. This did two things. First, it inflated the clients' egos. Second, it got the audience to buy that Pablo really did transform lives entirely, and that he could do the same for them.

It was painful for me to see people take bank loans in order to become Pablo's clients. I didn't want anything to do with such "sales" tactics myself, they disgusted me.

But there was clear proof, sadly, that they worked.

◆ ◆ ◆

DIARY ENTRY 39

The Darkest Hour Is Just before the Dawn

On and on the months went, working out insanely long days with Pablo.

I was thoroughly exhausted, in mind, body, and spirit.

But I was *not* a quitter.

I'd tell myself how much I was learning.

There was one week, somewhere around March 2018, where we had 10 events in six days in tours around Australia. We were so exhausted by the last tour, that none of us could deliver a single smile. Still, my boss was not happy, and now, I was pissed off. We scheduled a conversation, with my intention being to clarify that I would no longer accept the current situation.

It was not "ok" to work the insane hours we worked. It was not "ok" to sleep on the floor of the green room during breaks instead of in a proper hotel room. It was not "ok" to be told to look happy and receptive when we were exhausted. The conversation didn't work. My boss flipped the game and made *me* feel awful, telling me that *I* could make more effort, and that my complaints did not make sense.

I had, all this while, retained my mindset of gratitude.

I was *not* a quitter. I was no stranger to hard, backbreaking work, whether it was hard, physical labour or mind-numbing managerial work. I had worked as a waitress, I had worked scrubbing tables, I had worked frying potatoes ... remember? On my worst days, I had felt like a slave. But I had paid my dues.

I was *not* a quitter.

The emotional turmoil of wanting to quit but being unable to do so was profound.

It was maturity, anger, guilt, frustration, exhaustion, duty, and desire all rolled together. I could see the toll this work took on my well-being. I could see my heart longing for the thousands of alternative life paths I could choose instead of committing to this crazy organisation. Each day was like a delicate balancing act – I had to continue on the same path, with my game face on, while imagining another more fulfilling one.

On days that would have broken any normal human worker, I had reminded myself of my apartment by the beach, my life in Australia, my salary, my residency, the dreams I'd had back in Brazil ... and I convinced myself to stick around, working 20-hour days.

I was *not* a quitter.

I hope, for your sake, that such a time never comes in your career.

But if it does, remember that sometimes, things always seem to get worse right before they get a lot better. Or as the old English proverb goes: *"The darkest hour is just before the dawn."*

◆ ◆ ◆

DIARY ENTRY 40

Serendipity

Sometimes the universe won't give you what you want. It won't make things easier.

Sometimes, you might not even know exactly what to ask from the universe.

But the universe *will give you what you need*, if you let it.

At the beginning of 2018, when I was 33 years of old, while the days were crazy, I found myself the target of a marketing campaign about something called a "Remote Year".

A Remote Year was a year-long programme during which you lived in a different country every month. You needed to be selected for the programme to travel with a group of people.

Say what?!

By now, having worked with Pablo, I already knew what "being selected" meant – it was a sales tactic. So my job was to go to the selection interview and ask for a job instead. I mean someone would need to organise these trips, and who better to do it than me?

Obsessed, I reached out to apply, but no positions were open. I even made a video selling myself to the company, with recorded video recommendations from my friends from China. I worked on it for weeks, but to no avail.

I then started to think about how I could actually be one of the clients of Remote Year. The cost was $2K to get in, and another $2K per month for airfares and accommodation.

So, I went onto Google and typed: "How to make money online." And as I read the stuff that came up - about starting my own business, about becoming a designer or developer - a friend from my days in China called me.

We exchanged life updates, and she told me she was looking into the "Amazon Business". As I read more and more about the "Amazon Business," I discovered there were many ways to make money leveraging Amazon USA. All of them (at the time) involved selling physical products.

If you're taking notes, these are:

- **"Online retail arbitrage":** you buy a product cheaper somewhere else and sell it for a higher price on Amazon;
- **Wholesale selling:** you approach brands with good products and start selling them on Amazon (I could, say, sell products for the Brazilian gift company I worked for);
- **Private label product:** you find a product in high demand, with not too many competitors, and create your own brand on Amazon.

I found it all fascinating. In my mind until then, the only people who made a living online were designers and developers. Sure, there were other virtual assistant positions, but they paid very little per hour.

I was, at least for the time being, convinced that the only way I could make money online would be by opening my own business. This Amazon option clicked with me! That's what they call serendipity, right? Those unexpected, lucky discoveries ... those wonderful coincidences that lead us down magical new paths we didn't even know about!

I was reminded that day that we must live life wide-eyed, that the most transformative experiences can arise anytime, from anywhere.

◆ ◆ ◆

DIARY ENTRY 41

Me? A Businesswoman?

Have you ever found yourself doing something you never, ever thought you would do?

In my wildest imagination, I wouldn't have thought of being an entrepreneur – a businesswoman. Me? Start a business? I would have thought it was crazy. The subject always scared me - I was a proud and successful employee, and happy to be one. Employment is what I had always wanted, and always got.

There are many (good) reasons to choose the entrepreneurial path, but there are *also* many good reasons to work for someone else, including the certainty of having the money at the end of the month. The opportunity to use others' money to try out things. Personally, I never wanted to be a millionaire or anything – I was happy just to have the work, make my money, live comfortably and, of course, travel.

It was the seed of the possibility of travelling nonstop that had been planted in my mind, and that drove me to a large extent. We were in the day and age of remote work! Why could I not have that lifestyle for myself?

It seemed that destiny had wanted me to work for Pablo. His work intentions and ethics aside, the time I spent with him did make me think differently, and his talks were truly inspiring. Somehow, just organising his events, picking up things from his words, I started thinking more and more about the real possibility of starting my own business, and perhaps exploring how to make this "Amazon Business" thing work.

I started spending nights and weekends watching YouTube videos and researching coaches. Amongst several gurus, I found Leo Stanley; he would teach the very basics, for beginners. He had a podcast with success stories, mostly talking about retail and online arbitrage. I started waking up earlier to walk to work, just so I'd have some more time to listen to his podcast stories. The more I would hear, the more encouraged I would feel.

In a few months, I decided to try the business idea for real. I purchased Leo's online courses and was studying the ins and outs and techniques to find products for online arbitrage. In order to open an Amazon store, I needed to register a business in the USA. It seemed an easy task; I had the money, and 3 months later, I also had the EIN (Employer Identification Number).

And then began the trial and error.

If you're thinking of being an entrepreneur – I'd like to tell you upfront, be ready to fail, and start over, and fail, and start over, as many times as you need to. It is *only* through experimentation and first-hand learning that you uncover what really works. And you won't get there without being resilient, aggressive and determined.

I don't know if I can name any entrepreneur who was super successful from the very first idea or venture or project they had in mind. But I can name loads of them who failed BIG before their remarkable successes. Elon Musk struggled with E Zip2 and X.com (which later became PayPal). Nobody wanted to buy Colonel Sanders' secret recipe for fried chicken, and he eventually started his company (KFC), himself. Many people laughed at Brian Chesky, Joe Gebbia, and Nathan Blecharczyk when they said people would pay to live in other people's homes. And look at where AirBnB is today.

I could go on, but I think you get the gist. Entrepreneurship is *hard*, so just be ready.

Here's what my initial process looked like.

The first time I tried to sell something was in June 2018; I bought 5 superhero toys on the Walmart website, which I sent to my sister (who lives in the USA). She just needed to put a new barcode sticker on the product and ship to Amazon. Just in a week, the entire process was done, and my offer was live. I listed the product at $24, 3 times the cost price, and I sold each one of them in just 2 days!

The more I thought and heard about this, the more I believed in it, and I decided to sit with Pablo and ask him if I could leave the company. I was still waiting for my residency card, but we knew this would come in any minute.

My request to leave was not a shock for Pablo, who knew I was unhappy. Nonetheless, he did try to convince me to stay. In the end, we agreed I would work full-time for two more months, and then for another three months part-time. I also asked to go to the USA for a trip as Leo Stanley was giving a conference I wanted to be part of.

I couldn't wait. The world was going to become even smaller for me.

"By December 2018, I will be writing here in my diary from somewhere else in the world and I will be writing about how great is to be working remotely!" I wrote in my journal.

I had gotten used to - and even addicted to - this combination of emotions - fear, but with an internal belief that things will work out. The steadiness of business growth, but with my new dream of location independence.

It made me feel so alive!

◆ ◆ ◆

DIARY ENTRY 42

What Are Your Options?

I was happy, excited, and confident. I was in the USA for the Amazon Conference.

And then, out of the blue, I received a call from Pablo in Australia.

It was unusual for him to call me while I was on a break, so I already sensed something was off and picked up the phone straight away.

"It's about your Australia Residency Card. It was denied."

My voice disappeared. My head went everywhere. My heart started racing. It felt like I was hit by a sudden burst of ice-cold wind, that left me frozen, disoriented, and in pain.

The world around me stopped turning, but my mind was trying to process the piece of information I had just received.

WHAT? How could this be possibly happening? I was so confident, and my case was so strong! I *knew* my case was strong! Perhaps the lawyers had done something wrong? I was utterly lost, and that was maybe one of the saddest days of my life.

Following this unexpected blow, I was forced to confront the harsh reality, but my head would not stop spinning.

If that news hadn't been enough, I also received the harsh reminder notice that I had just 30 days to leave the country. I was in the USA right now, I would return to Australia in two weeks, which meant I had TWO WEEKS to return to Australia and move away. This was insane!

There was one alternative: to appeal the decision. The cost was $15K, and I would get an extra 18 months in the country.

I took a few deep breaths to digest the options I had, and to make note of the pros and cons of each. I think it's the best way to process my thoughts when I'm in a fix.

Option 1:

I could make my boss pay for the re-application process, and then work full-time for him for some extra months. But this would mean I would not have time to work on my business at all, plus I would have to travel for the events and "suck it up" when it came to all the stress.

Option 2:

I could pay for the process myself. Work just part-time and focus on my business. But, for God's sake, this would mean spending the $15K from my pocket.

I took a step back to assess everything, seeking the path that made the most sense, weighing the risks and rewards. I reluctantly (but practically) decided to go with Option 1.

Was it what I really wanted? Probably not. I did not want to stay in my comfort zone. I did not want to stay stuck and unhappy. But to be honest, I was also afraid. I was afraid of taking too long to learn the Amazon Business for real, of not being good enough in the business world, of making wrong decisions, of sabotaging myself, of not making enough money.

And my logical brain also accepted that I absolutely could not consider leaving Australia in just two weeks – that would be crazy. I did not have much in savings, and just leaving the country abruptly would be a very painful option for me. I was counting on a few more months of working to build up some savings.

I finished the conference (which was very inspiring), and I got back to Australia and sat down with Pablo to discuss our possibilities.

I think Pablo thought I would surely not leave Australia without my residency card, but I told him that I was firm in my decision to leave him. Yes, I needed more time in the country but I absolutely would not agree to stay an extra 18 months. He then said he would pay for the appeal, and in return, he wanted me to work full-time for another 5 months.

The time passed quickly! As I had known, I had no time to work on my business. But at least I did save up a few dollars. My plan was to go to Brazil first, spend Christmas once again with family, move to the USA for three months and then Europe.

In my head, I wanted to use those three months in the USA to focus on studying the Amazon Business: specifically, how to do retail arbitrage from there. I would also learn how to build a brand and perhaps sell my own products. I knew it would take time to build up my business and start making good money. My plan was to move somewhere in Europe with a cheap cost of living for another six months (I was envisioning making around $2K per month with my business). And then, eventually, make good enough money ($4K+) to be completely free and travel to wherever I wanted.

To my surprise, things turned out way better than I even dreamt of.

◆ ◆ ◆

DIARY ENTRY 43

If You Never Try, You'll Never Know

Let me tell you now: entrepreneurship is not for the faint-hearted.

It will extract from you the greatest strength of spirit and an overwhelming sense of responsibility. Sure, there's passion, and excitement, and the freedom of being your own boss. But there's also the darkness of the unknown, there's doubt and insecurity, and the heavy weight of taking on everything on your own two shoulders. And I don't know how comfortable you are with "putting yourself out there," but as an entrepreneur, you will need to, and this takes some work if you're a shy person. You need the right opportunities, the right people, the right partners, investors, clients, employees, vendors, designers, programmers, and more and more people *to find you*.

The rewards are there – but they will come in their own time.

All in all, there is tremendous personal growth, the satisfaction of having "gone for it" when millions of others won't, and the chance of being able to truly create something from the ground up.

During my USA stint, I tried, and failed, and tried, and failed, and tried again.

I had decided to live with a friend from my China days (we actually took a short cruise together between Miami and the Bahamas and connected in a romantic way). I chose to live with him, have fun, and pursue the possibility of falling in love, rather than stay with my sister, which was my other option. I also decided to invest some more money in coaching. $4K was a lot for me at the time, but something I thought would be needed to speed up the process.

It didn't. The only valuable tip I picked up was about Trader Joe's, an American chain of grocery stores that weren't all across the USA, but were there in Iowa, where I was.

And I began my journey to set up a viable venture on Amazon.

Attempt 1: I started buying a bunch of food (from Trader Joe's and Walmart) and selling it on Amazon. It would always sell fast. Everything I would buy, I would eventually sell. But after the product cost, the shipping cost and the Amazon fee factored in, I was not making a profit.

Attempt 2: I tried to crack the code for keyword research. When it comes to having a private label, and having your own brand, you need to know what people are looking for already. Keywords help you stand out as selling things people would want. I'd buy things from China and list them on Amazon. But those would never sell ...

Attempt 3: What actually put some money in my pocket was something else my coach told me about: diabetic strips. These were in very high demand and cost a fortune in pharmacies. And there were many old people receiving these from the government for free, probably as part of some health insurance, or because they were related to someone who had passed on. In Iowa, there were many old people, so I'd drive all over, find them, buy their box of strips for $10, and sell these on eBay for $50 or $60 depending on the condition of the box. These sales would happen right away! It was very lucrative. Demand and supply, right? But there were only so many people I could find to buy the strips from. Plus, I figured this wasn't sustainable, and I couldn't move this model online.

Meanwhile, my life with my friend was chaotic. He was a party animal and would get drunk daily, we'd fight a lot, and I'd get distracted from my business. I was tired of playing "housewife" alone, cooking lunches and dinners and house cleaning.

In time, I moved to my sister's and got an air ticket to Portugal. My plan was to go to Europe, and I would not change that. If anything, I had started to accept the possibility that I might have to find a normal job again, but in Europe.

I had 30 days before moving to Portugal, I wasn't making much on Amazon, and started to get anxious and desperate.

Ok, time for **Attempt 4**.

I once again began by going to Google to ask, "how to make money online".

This time, I found a course on how to open a social media management agency. I disliked the idea, but I was desperate! I needed to start making money, and preferably online. I had no money - my sister helped by gifting me $1,000, and the course had cost $500.

At the beginning of the course, the teacher mentioned the freelancer platform, "Upwork". I had heard of it, and that's where I had hired some VA's back in the day. But this time around, he was teaching us how to find *clients* on Upwork.

(If you are interested to know how, jump on my Instagram @lufistarol and get my mini course "Finding Remote Work". For way less than I paid, I will teach you how to do the same.)

Ok, **Attempt 5**.

If I don't keep trying, how will I know what works and what doesn't?

So just for fun, I decided to type in "Amazon" on Upwork. And behold! I encountered a job offer from an agency looking for an "Online Business Manager."

An online business manager? What on earth? The job description articulated they needed someone, preferably located in Europe, preferably with knowledge of the Amazon Seller Central, preferably with experience of managing a team, preferably with a guarantee of execution ...

I was smiling so hard, and I was so thoroughly happy, that I almost cried. They were looking for ME! I had been playing with Amazon Seller Central for the past 3 months. I had managed teams my entire life. They were looking for me!

Five attempts, and I had finally found something that worked. It may not have been exactly what I was looking for, but perhaps it was something even better.

I was going to Europe.

◆ ◆ ◆

DIARY ENTRY 44

Becoming a Digital Nomad (Finally!)

Getting the Europe role meant I was going to be getting paid to learn the Amazon game. I could live there, work, learn, and build my own business on the side.

I had applied for the job on Upwork - I found the name of the lady that had posted the opening and got in touch with her on Facebook and on LinkedIn, informing her I was their best bet, and asking her to please interview me.

For me, interview = job offer, 100% of the time! That's why interviews are so important. Get the interview. Get face to face, and you've won the battle – at least most of it.

Four days later, I got a call for an interview, and I spoke to the owners.

Even before we spoke about money, I was in. (I had my growth formula in my back pocket: prove your worth and then ask for more – it never fails). Luckily for me, they offered $4,000 per month, which was much more than the $2,000 I was budgeting for.

I was so happy I lied to her in the interview about moving to Europe, and I said I was moving there the very next week. Once I had the offer, the first thing I did was bring forward my flight. I would let nothing take an opportunity like this away from me.

And that was the beginning of my Digital Nomad lifestyle: I would be working as an Online Business Manager for an amazing start-up that helps e-commerce business owners succeed on Amazon. My bosses were inspiring American entrepreneurs. My team was spread all around the world, and my office was wherever there was internet. Seriously, I was over the moon! I was going to be a truly globetrotting digital business executive!

Things like #believe, #makeithappen and #europe weren't just Instagram hashtags to daydream about anymore - I was going to live that life.

I did land in Portugal soon, but went to travel for work almost immediately, first to the UK. I met the girl who was leaving, Maria, who introduced me to everyone and everything.

I distinctly remember learning how the time of remote employees was controlled digitally with software that logged work hours and took screenshots of their computers. I also remember hearing about how the agency had helped one client reach a revenue on Amazon of around $100K per month, and finding the number high. I remember how happy Maria was when I started to bring new ideas and forms of execution.

Satisfied with my work and my meetings so far, I returned to Portugal.

During my weekends, I would rent a car and drive around and explore the country. On weekdays, I would work. They had wanted someone in Europe to be online 9–5 in that time zone, and I had *several* meetings during the day.

I was enjoying it. But, seeing the bad results the agency was bringing to clients, as well as hearing complaints from the team members, I started to get a little scared about my prospects. What if this start-up fails and I lose my job? Out of worry that I might soon have to look for a job again, I went onto Upwork, and updated my profile to an "Amazon seller agency" myself, listing my services about how I could help Amazon sellers. I could take care of everything with regards to an Amazon Store. I didn't have much intention behind the change of profile, just leaving it there in case I needed to plug into a "Plan B", and find somewhere else to work.

And I left it at that.

After two months in Portugal, I was thinking, why am I still here? I am free to travel!

I found another group only that offered a programme similar to the Remote Year. This one was called Hackers Paradise. After some application work and some more logistics hassles, I found myself in *Italy*, for a month that turned out to be eye-opening.

There were so many people who had normal jobs, but who were working them online! There were your usual designers and programmers, but there were also your not-so-usual human resources recruiters, pharmaceutical researchers ...

Some of them needed to work 9:00 am to 5:00 pm in the USA time zone, which meant starting work in Europe from around 8:00 pm. And most of them were not locked in time zones at all. They would choose when they worked, and use the daylight hours to go to the beach, learn how to cook, explore a winery ... I would have loved to join them, but my working hours really were 9 to 5 Europe time, and I honoured those. I was jealous and truly wanted to participate in the activities, but I was still extremely grateful for having remote work and being part of the group.

For now, this broadening of my horizons, this new way of looking at work and at life, and seeing how real it was, how *normal* it was, was enough.

* If you want to apply for the Hackers Paradise programme, mention my name to them for a $100 discount on your first trip

◆ ◆ ◆

DIARY ENTRY 45

When One Door Shuts ...

I was, once again, flourishing at work.

The clients were loving my services, and my bosses were so happy I had their trust. Those reporting to me were happy as well and mentioned things like *"I finally know how the work I am doing affects everybody else's work"*, or *"I feel more like I'm part of a team now!"* which to me was a MASSIVE win as a manager.

Just three months in, the company owners invited me to go with them to a big Amazon conference in the USA. They also wanted to take the opportunity to talk about the future and the company's growth. The idea was for us to be reunited for three days, then go to the conference.

I flew from Italy to Los Angeles, took a taxi, met the company CEO at his house, and went to sleep.

The next morning, at 7:00 am, the other company CEO arrived and, as planned, both CEOs and I were to have breakfast. The agenda was for us to talk about myself and my position. I had decided to take this opportunity to ask for an in-depth review and feedback of my services, with the intention of then asking for an increase in my salary.

It started with them asking me what I thought about the company, and I had my speech prepared. I showed them the numbers, the efficiency I had brought to the company, pointed out areas of improvement. I had learnt by then, from a lot of experience in the corporate world, that you need to *announce what you are doing*. This will be most important on those days when people don't know what you are doing. You've got to figure out how to make yourself visible. Personally, I think it helps to create dashboards where others can see exactly how and where you are bringing evolution to the company.

Ok, now it was their turn to speak, so I asked what they thought about me.

What happened next made time stop. The lady CEO opened her computer, turned the screen to me and asked, *"What is this?"* She was pointing to my Upwork profile – the one I had created long ago to position myself as an "Amazon agency." I didn't know exactly how Upwork worked – I had created the profile and clicked a button to say that I was NOT available for work, for the profile to NOT be visible, but perhaps Upwork makes new profiles visible anyway?

My profile was very much "online," and to make things even worse, it mentioned I was "available to work from 24th June 2019," which was the **exact** date the Amazon conference was ending.

After this, there was absolutely no way for me to convince the owners of the truth. I spoke my heart out – my feelings at the beginning of the role, the negative feedback from the rest of the team, my initial doubts of leaving ... they wouldn't hear it. They didn't care. In the lady's mind, I was "using" her company to steal her team members, to steal her clients, and to be sponsored for the Amazon event where I could make my own personal connexions.

In her mind, I wasn't trustworthy. In her mind, there was no option but to fire me.

They knew I had a sister in Florida, so they just purchased a flight ticket for me to go to Florida. They did not allow me to even put my feet inside the house again; off I was to Florida, my flight just six hours away.

I was in a state of semi-shock. I remember arriving at the airport, sitting on the floor and staring at the wall. I think I sat there for at least three hours. How had I been so stupid? How had I managed to find remote work, with a great salary, and ruin it? What had just happened?

My sister and her family weren't even home; luckily, they had a passcode system to open the door and I let myself in. The next day I was still trying to digest what happened. I received a zillion documents from the company lawyers saying that everything I knew about the company was official and confidential, that if I breached anything they would take legal action. It was so much drama, I could not believe it.

By the next day, I sort of began accepting the situation, and focusing on going back to Upwork to find something else for myself.

In the following days, I applied for all the jobs you can imagine.

Honestly – if you ever try this for the first time – your mind will be blown away by the type of job opportunities you find. My job hunting on Upwork had started with the mindset of there being possibilities everywhere. And really, there were.

I wrote to over 50 positions in a five-day job search window. I interviewed with four:

- A company that organised bus trips around Europe for young people needing help with planning;
- A new business coach needing a project manager to keep the team on track;
- Another coach who was just starting out as a speaker needing operations assistance after the deal was sealed; and
- An Amazon seller needing help to control his inventory.

Interview = job offer, right? Right!

All of them offered me a job.

All were paying by the hour, and were expecting me to work around 30 hours per week, except for the Amazon guy, James, who I figured would need just 2 or 3 hours per week. He was paying only $18 per hour, which was a lower rate than the others.

I'm not sure what it was that made me go for the James opportunity. I guess it was that I had invested so much time and money to learn about the Amazon business, that I wanted to continue to be connected to it. I didn't want to go backwards into events or into dealing with the big egos of coaches. Additionally, by then, I had already learnt how to recognise the potential for growth in an Upwork client.

This guy had spent more than $50K on talent on Upwork, which means he was hiring people all the time. I just sensed I could grow in the company. Plus, I liked him. I liked his vibe.

Our "interview" was actually more like a conversation, and he opened up to me about more brands, and about more responsibilities I could possibly take on. He told me that in 1 or 2 years I could even be hiring a team to help me out.

It wasn't just a sales pitch – I believed in this growth. So I decided to say "yes" only to him. I already knew that there was a sea of opportunities out there, and if I needed money, I could always take on some other jobs.

I left the USA with my new work contract in hand, and headed to my next destination: Berlin, Germany.

I've mentioned this many times in this book, but I really want to get you to believe it: If you come across work where you think you can make a difference, *accept it*. Don't just look at how much they will pay you. Believe in yourself. Trust that you will make a jump, and another, and another. Know that because you like that work, and that opportunity, you are more likely to overdeliver. And that the value you offer will translate into your negotiation power.

I have worked all over the world, and this method of growth has never failed me.

◆ ◆ ◆

DIARY ENTRY 46

Beyond Gratitude

Finally, with this role, I would get to experience the life of co-living.

In some co-living arrangements, the minimum you can stay for is three months, and my contract was with a firm that had three buildings in three different locations.

I picked one in Moabit: a four-storey building with four apartments on each floor, each one with four rooms, two bathrooms, and a shared kitchen. My apartment had two guys from Costa Rica, one of them with a girlfriend from Ecuador. The fourth room had a constant change of people. The Costa Ricans, the lady and I became good friends almost instantly. I also made other friends from the same building: a gay South Korean guy, another Mexican guy, and I had a brief romance with a neighbour originally from Germany. Friends from my days in China came to visit me in Berlin. All in all, it was a very fun three months, full of parties, exploration, swimming naked in the lakes, riding bicycles around, going to museums, partying at famous nightclubs.

No matter where you are in the world, and how obsessed with your work you are, friendships *matter*. A full social life helps you maintain your sanity in all areas of your life, including work.

At work, as you've seen from my life countless times, there are ebbs and flows. There are shocks, both good and bad. And there's steady sailing - again, both good and bad. But you learn that the tide always turns.

At work, in the first two weeks I started, James, the CEO, was changing the supplier for his best-selling product. Because I had come to take care of inventory, he started copying me into the emails. The supplier was Chinese and, reading the thread, I didn't find a single instance when James had tried to negotiate prices. I then asked him if I could please interfere. In fact, I asked him, *"James, how much do you want to pay for this product?"*

At the time, he was paying the old supplier $1.85, and this new supplier was quoting $1.75. He was already happy. But sensing the excitement of a challenge, he told me that if I could grab it for $1.60, he would be extremely happy. I smiled: was he really thinking this was a challenge? Perhaps he didn't remember - I had lived and worked in China for years. I asked him to stay cool, because a Chinese negotiation will close at the moment you feel you are going to lose the supplier - *but he'll always come back*.

Luckily for me, James did his job and didn't intervene. And I ended up getting the product price down to $1.35.

This was something the company was buying 100,000 units of per year (and we buy about 300,000 now). Which meant that as soon as I joined, I saved him more than $40K.

How impressed he was!

During the two weeks of negotiation, I was also presented to his dad, who was taking care of the inventory. Two products were being bought from China, and the rest were manufactured in the USA. All the components (boxes and bottles) came from China as well. There were three warehouses. It was very complex, with information and numbers spread everywhere.

I made a new spreadsheet, using the exact same formulas he would use to predict inventory purchases, but I made it more visual. Then, I automated the dashboard generation.

The time for our calculations was reduced significantly, and I was just asking for more and more work to do. The more work I would ask for, the more I would receive. With every task, I would see room for improvement - automate, make it faster, and free up valuable time.

In just three weeks of being employed by James, I was now doing some 20 hours per week, but it was still not enough. He asked me what I wanted. And I said that I wanted more work. I confessed that the number I was seeking was $4K per month, and that if he matched that number, I would not need to go find work elsewhere.

He said yes!

I was worried about continuing to track my time - after all, he was paying me for 40 hours per week of employment, and I wanted to prove I was doing that time. He didn't have a time tracker. Even more surprisingly, he didn't even care. I made one, and gave him access, but he never asked to see it. I just need to have two meetings with him per week, and that was it.

So there we go – within three weeks of the whole being fired episode, I was already working for somebody else, had the equivalent of a full-time job, *and* had the freedom of the timing I wanted to work.

I understood - finally – that sometimes bad things happen to you, like being suddenly fired. And those things make you feel like you've lost the ground beneath you. You might not even know why they happened.

I'll tell you why they happen: to make room for something more amazing and magical to occur.

In hindsight, you are mostly left with gratitude. You just have to stay positive. You just have to stay curious.

When I look back today, I am thoroughly happy with the incident that got me get fired.

I am, in general, so good at my work that nobody would ever fire me. That unlucky coincidence of my profile showing up on Upwork was luck in disguise; I had been asking the Universe for work with more flexible hours, and that is exactly what it wanted to give me.

I was beyond grateful.

◆ ◆ ◆

DIARY ENTRY 47

A Whole New World

Fast forward just one year, and the organisation was constantly growing, in revenue as well as in team members. Before I knew it, I was managing a team of ten.

Continue to know what you're worth, and continue to ask for it ... As my responsibilities increased, so did my fixed fee.

Every three months, for the first two years, I found myself negotiating a new fee increase (each time for at least an extra 30%).

A lot of people I know, digital nomads and street corner office executives alike, keep waiting for the "right time" to negotiate a pay hike. They wait for the start of the next year, they wait for Christmas, they wait for their boss to be in a "good mood", they wait for the company's "salary hike time," or they wait till they "feel" ready. And unfortunately, they miss several chances to negotiate – and they remain in a situation of financial scarcity, living uncomfortably.

Don't wait.

Of course, the prerequisite is hard work. But with hard work, you can use my formula repeatedly to get a pay rise, as many times a year as you want. The harder you work, the more confident you become. And the more confident you become, the better you can get paid.

If there's another big lesson I've learnt from eventually finding the digital nomad life, it is that you can succeed, monetarily and otherwise, and you can do so *on your terms*.

Often, in no small part due to the social narratives surrounding us, we start to develop a very limited, stereotypical way of thinking.

Want to make a lot of money? You need to be working 60+ hours a week on Wall Street. Want to spend your life as a designer? Forget about making big bucks.

It takes courage to explore new ways of thinking. But once you do open up your mind, you'll see how abundant the world is.

Remember Clara, the Brazilian lady who gave me work in China? She was also my friend and I would tell her about this magnificent remote work world I had stepped into.

I soon started hiring her for some freelance work here and there in the design department, and with her background, she grew in no time to manage our Creative Department, with a salary way above that of her VP role, while working flexible hours from the comfort of her home and leading a team of seven designers.

Broaden your horizons. It is only in your mind that you've built so many limitations. I marvelled at my own growth the more my own horizons expanded – not just in terms of the money I was earning, but in who I was becoming, as a person, as a manager and as a leader.

Working for James and the Novak family was game-changing. I was at first clocking in 35 hours of work per week. Side note here: When you work in an office, work hours include time for coffee, time chatting with colleagues ... but when you're clocking in hours digitally, it's just pure work, all of it. So trust me when I say 35 hours of logged-in work a week is quite a lot! I was used to hard work, but I was not used to the care I got. James would notice me stressed and overwhelmed, and he would tell me to relax. To do *less*.

He would *help*.

And I was, as I mentioned, developing entirely different paradigms of thinking. When you adapt to new models of work, you've got to be ready to stop thinking in the old way. For instance, consider the hiring process we followed. It was the same deal: I hire you by the hour, if you're good, your price per hour increases. If you're great, we work with you on a fixed fee basis. When people were working by the hour, I would use the time control tool to check how much I needed to pay them, and to see their screenshots for proof of how much they were actually working. Even if we later hired them full-time, I would make them use the time control software to complete at least 35 hours of work per week. This was my old way of thinking, until I realised: why do this? If they can complete their work in 10 hours per week instead of 35, good for them! I transformed myself and started thinking like James. I stopped caring about the amount of time they worked. All I cared about was the results they were bringing.

When I became less – shall we say *obsessive* – about their working hours, I also started caring more about what was going on in their personal lives, because I realised that it makes a big influence on your deliverables.

James taught me to trust people, and to be more human. And I'm so glad!

There's an excellent quote by Stephen Covey we should remember, at work and in life: *"Trust is the glue of life. It's the foundational principle that holds all relationships."*

I remember a few situations that blew my mind. In my second year in the company, we were growing faster than expected. We had already increased the salary of the freelancers twice, but James just looked at me and said: "Ok, but the company is doing more now. I want to increase their fixed rate again." I had never seen a CEO offering higher salaries – I had always seen it go the other way.

Next, James offered the three of us - the first ones to join the team - a part of the company. Sure, it was a smart move, a way to guarantee we would stick around longer. But it made us feel like owners, too, and that's a whole new feeling. Over a timeframe of five years, for example, I'd gain something like 0.075% of the company (which I would negotiate later to be more like 1%).

There were multiple such examples, but for the most part, I think it was just the fact that James and his family would be *human* first, and money-makers later, that made a mark on me. I had worked all over the world, but I had never seen this attitude.

There was another situation where I had brought in a brilliant friend of mine from Brazil to work with us. He was by far the smartest and best person I knew at building spreadsheets in the entire world, and a dear friend. We brought him on as a freelancer, and I later convinced James to hire him.

Three months went by, and he was simply not delivering due to personal issues. I would argue with him all the time. I started feeling embarrassed for bringing him on, and I went to the Novak family thinking we may have to let him go, but the first set of questions in their minds were: *"What can we do to help? Does he live with somebody else? Does he have family looking after him?"*

That attitude was what I was in love with – I wanted it to shape me. I wanted to be an advocate for letting people be free to do the work on their own time.

I wanted to love life, and live it well – and I wanted the same for others, because when we truly do that, we show up even better at work.

◆ ◆ ◆

DIARY ENTRY 48

Good Roots, Bad Roots

I kept living the best life I could – or at least trying to.

In October 2021 I wanted to go the mountains. I was scrolling social media when I saw a post of a German guy I had met while Coworking & Coliving in Morocco, and he was asking people where he should go next. I went to check the answers, as I was also researching where to go next.

I saw someone commenting he should go to Bansko, Bulgaria. They were organising an event called, "The Women in the Mountains". I clicked on the link, which opened a Facebook page about this event, which showed a picture of a small city surrounded by magnificent mountains. It was for an entire month, sharing a chalet, having my own private ensuite room and it was just 600 Euros. I did not even think twice, and off I was!

At the event, I met Alexa, who worked with hypnotherapy. I had always found hypnotherapy fascinating, and I became extremely curious. She told me she could remove any blocks I had and implant positive things in my subconscious mind.

I was, at the time in a kind of suffering. You could say I had imposter syndrome: I felt like I was still not worthy of the money I was making. After all, my entire life I had worked really hard. I had worked weekends, I had worked long hours. How was possible for me to be making so much money working this little? This was my block.

Very soon, we were going to have a big Amazon promo and I knew the company would grow, and so would my money, through commissions. In my mind, I was not deserving of it.

I decided to work with Alexa and have this block addressed in one session of hypnotherapy. I was both excited and terrified.

In the session, amongst the many memories that came up, there was one from Apiuna when I had wanted to go and play with Dad, and Mum wouldn't let me because I had not done the housework ... It was there. Even after all these years, travels, life, and work all around the world, it was still there.

The message that became apparent to me then is that, in my subconscious mind, I kept linking extremely hard work to any kind of reward. As a child, the reward had been playtime. As an adult, it was money. Without hard work, I would not be deserving – or so I had come to think.

And so, for the remainder of the session, we worked around that. For 21 days, I listened to a hypnosis recording that helped shift my mindset completely.

In addition to this, my practice of reflection and journaling helped me arrive at a clearer way of thinking.

The money we make is not for the hours we work, or for the hours we prove we work. In fact, it's more correct to think that the money we make is for our *knowledge*.

Knowledge comes from many things and shows itself in many ways. It showed in my rapid decision-making, in my capacity to solve issues before they even arose, and in my ability to keep calm when there was a storm.

You are worthy, and it is necessary to recognise that you're worthy. All you know, all you bring to the table, *matters*.

When I got back to work, I not only charged what I was supposed to, but a few months down the road, I once again negotiated my salary, jumping another 50%.

The subconscious mind is a powerful force, capable of shaping our behaviour without our realising it. Have you ever thought you could have some trauma which is blocking you from achieving your greatest potential? There is no shame in seeking professional help to unlock your potential. Whether through coaching or hypnosis, remarkable results can be achieved.

* If you are interested in hypnotherapy and want to contact Alexa, send me a private message on Instagram: @lufistarol.

◆ ◆ ◆

DIARY ENTRY 49

The Mysteries of a Life Without Borders

Diving into the world as a digital nomad is like embarking on a journey where the destination is shaped by our own choices and desires. The concept of "home" becomes elusive; it's no longer tied to a fixed address, but rather a state of mind, a connection with the world, and the people we meet along the way.

Many inquire about the challenges of this life. "How do you handle constant change?", "Isn't it lonely?", "How do you maintain relationships?". I respond with a smile: being a digital nomad is a deliberate choice for freedom and continuous learning.

Understanding Digital Nomadism:
For many, being nomadic is synonymous with instability. But in my experience, this instability is balanced by a rich sense of freedom. Waking up and deciding that today will be a workday by the sea in Thailand or perhaps a coffee shop in enchanting Budapest is a luxury few experience.

Relationships on the Road:
Yes, maintaining relationships can be challenging. But at the same time, each city, each country offers an opportunity to forge new bonds. Moreover, the digital nomad life has fostered a global community. Nearly everywhere I go, I find a familiar face or someone who met someone I know. It's a web of connections that weaves around the world.

Debunking the Myths:
A common misconception is that digital nomads are forever lonely, detached, and shun commitments. The truth is more nuanced. Many of us yearn for deep and lasting connections. Circumstances might shift, but the inherent human desire to belong endures.

Money and Personal Worth:
There's a tendency to believe that nomadism is an escape from financial responsibilities. In reality, the freedom of being a nomad comes with understanding the value of money as a tool. A tool that allows us to invest in experiences, personal growth, and, most importantly, our own well-being.

Throughout this journey, I've learned that worth isn't just in the money we earn, but in the knowledge we gain and share, the experiences we live, and the stories we tell.

The True Essence of Nomadic Life:
To me, being a digital nomad is more than just traveling. It's a life philosophy. It's about accepting impermanence, embracing uncertainty, and being open to the endless possibilities the world offers. It's about finding beauty in every nook, learning from every culture, and building bridges instead of walls.

Ultimately, being a digital nomad is a journey of self-discovery. With each new destination, we learn more about ourselves and the world around us. And in doing so, we find that although the scenery might change, the quest for meaning, connection, and growth is universal.

Thus, I encourage everyone to question, explore, and dive deep into the vast ocean of opportunities life presents. Because, in the end, it's not the places we visit, but the experiences we live and the people we meet along the way that shape who we are.

◆ ◆ ◆

DIARY ENTRY 50

No Borders, Just Horizons

I often think about Amelia Earhart. She was the first woman aviator to fly solo across the Atlantic, and she was also a writer. She used to say, "No borders, just horizons ... Only freedom."

When I look back at my dreams as a child in Brazil, and I open my eyes to see my life right now, there is one overwhelming feeling: gratitude.

I work for mind-blowing, inspiring, caring people who let me work the way I want and from anywhere I want.

I don't know if you know that just 10% of American households make more than 6 figures per year - and I'm grateful and proud to be included in this group, while shaping my life on my terms.

Still, life is asking me to outgrow myself once again. I am once again taking the courage to leave a very comfortable set up with my current company and go pursue a more fulfilling career. That's why, this time, I decided to write this book. I decided to share my knowledge and life lessons to hopefully inspire people to take action towards their dreams.

I learnt from my journey exactly how to grow in every role, in position and in salary, and I've taught you my formulas. My own career path taught me how to repeatedly negotiate – to ask for whatever it was that I wanted, whether it was money, time, education, travel or all four.

It is now my mission to show people what is possible. It is my mission to convince others to break the mental blocks they've grown up with about what it takes to succeed. It is my mission to bust countless myths that keep us from wealth, from knowledge, from growth, from love, and from the best lives we can live. All we need to do is show up, with an intention to make a difference.

There are no borders in our new world, just more horizons. And freedom is calling again.

If you are interested in working with me, you can see my offerings at: linktr.ee/lufistarol.

For now, I sign off, and I hope to cross paths with you someday, in some beautiful corner of this endless world. In the meantime, I wish for you every blessing, every form of growth, and every adventure your heart desires.

Notes

Made in the USA
Middletown, DE
22 October 2023